ME AND MY VA

ARE YOU READY TO LEVERAGE YOUR BUSINESS WITH A VIRTUAL ASSISTANT?

NATASA DENMAN
LENDY MACARIO

First published by Ultimate World Publishing 2020
Copyright © 2020 Natasa Denman & Lendy Macario

ISBN
Paperback - 978-1-922372-14-7
Ebook - 978-1-922372-15-4

Cover design: Ultimate World Publishing
Layout and typesetting: Ultimate World Publishing
Editor: Marinda Wilkinson

Ultimate World Publishing
Diamond Creek,
Victoria Australia 3089
www.writeabook.com.au

Dedication

Natasa Denman

I dedicate this book to all the busy business owners, that are ready to let go and leverage their business with a virtual assistant. You will wonder why you didn't do it earlier. All the best and here's to your business success!!!

To Lendy, thank you for being always there, willing to learn and grow with the business. I could not ask for a better virtual assistant!

To my family, for accepting Lendy as an integral part of what we do and how we do it. We get to live a wonderfully balanced lifestyle and know the business is looked after, especially while we travel.

Lendy Macario

I would like to dedicate this book to my family, Ultimate 48 Hour Author team and my partner. To all aspiring virtual assistants, this book is also for you. My journey of being a VA has been amazing and I would like to thank everyone who has inspired me.

Contents

Introduction

Natasa Denman

We boarded our flight from the island of Boracay in the Philippines to start our homeward bound trip to Melbourne. I had just spent eight days on this beautiful island for our annual conference with my personal assistant Viv, my virtual assistant Lendy and my mum (my bookkeeper, postie and all round awesome grandma to my three kids whom she is in charge of when my husband Stuart and I have to get on a flight and execute our business trips and tours). During the one-hour flight to Manila, we reminisced, discussing how great we felt about the whole team, the productivity of the conference and the bonding that we experienced in the Philippines.

What we do and how we do it is not easy, and I often get comments from those that have followed my journey on how well organised and responsive our whole team is. Yet we still have wonderfully balanced lives and are not exhausted at the end of each working day. Instead, we feel fulfilled and purposeful. We know each other's strengths and weaknesses and understand how they fit into the picture of the business as a whole.

So, on that quick one-hour flight, we realised something – how we support each other works, and this may be of value to other business owners out there. So many try to do everything themselves (I was one of them) and end up exhausted, resentful and worse. They lack financial stability in their business and are stretched, doing many daily tasks they should be delegating, so they can focus on the big stuff.

My VA Lendy and I have been together for the past four years. She was the first virtual assistant I spoke to and I trained her from scratch. We've built a great working and personal relationship which continues to develop, and I can see her being part of our team for many more years to come.

Even though you may be thinking someone with more experience around virtual assistants should write this book (and they should), I believe wholeheartedly that our story is unique and carries a ton of value for those that lack experience as a business owner seeking a VA and a VA looking to do this type of work – just like Lendy and I. She had never had a VA job before, and I had never had a VA before her. We tested and trialled steps, actions and systems. We learnt what worked, without advice or help from anyone else. Maybe we were just lucky, maybe we happened to be the perfect match for one another or maybe, just maybe we intuitively worked out a system that worked for us. I am 100% certain that sharing the things we do daily, weekly, monthly and on an annual basis will help many entrepreneurs have successful, productive and (importantly) long-term relationships with their VAs.

First though, here's a little more of my story including some mistakes I made before hiring Lendy. As I write this book, I am about to celebrate a decade in my business. A multiple seven-figure business that is fully run from home by family, aside from my PA and VA who have now become very much like family. We built this up to provide a wonderful lifestyle for our three children (Judd, Mika and Xara), to travel the world, and to have an impact on the lives of others, who have a desire to do the same for themselves and their families.

The vehicle that drives this mission is Ultimate 48 Hour Author and Ultimate World Publishing. We help first-time authors bring their book to reality via our retreats. Nowadays, we also continue helping them publish their second, third and fourth books – and beyond. It took me three years of trial and error as a life coach to come up with my signature system that is Ultimate 48 Hour Author. I was a weight loss coach, product development coach and a generic small business coach. I also had a go at licensing some of my programs to leverage one to many.

I networked a lot, spoke at events and kept testing various programs, masterminds and online trainings, until one day I realised that people wanted to model what I had created for myself. To this day, every book I release, every program I provide and everything I teach, comes purely from reverse engineering what I have done successfully for myself. I was the one that wrote a book in a weekend first and that is why I thought I could show others how to do it for themselves. Every time I hear someone ask me a question multiple times, I start to see that there is a need out there to provide the answer. The answers are no good living just in my head when others can benefit from them. Why deny people a shortcut you know that can make their lives easier?

This book is exactly that. The answer to the multiple times I have been asked these questions over the years:

- How did you find your VA?
- How do you pay her?
- What does your VA do for you?
- How do you train her?
- What if she makes a mistake?
- What systems do you guys use?

Here's the thing. I did not have a VA for the first six years of running my business, however I did have a SD (a Stuart Denman). My husband quit his day job two and a half years after I started the business. Before that I was doing everything myself and still managed to grow a six-figure business. If I knew how to work smarter, I should have hired my VA before I hired my husband – it would have been much cheaper and easier to get the business to the next level. I should have hired a VA once I started getting paying clients. But no, I was scared. I thought, if I can't pay myself, how can I afford to pay a complete stranger?

Here are some of my fears that you may recognise in yourself as you consider embarking on this path:

- I can't possibly afford a VA
- What would I give them to do – I can do it all myself
- Do I have enough regular hours for a VA?
- I haven't written any systems, I am not ready
- Will they represent my brand well?
- Will their English be good enough?
- What if they stuff up?

- Can I really let go of stuff? (after all most business owners are control freaks).

These fears controlled my mind for years. I am lucky to be blessed with a very organised gene (or maybe my mum is responsible for that one), so I still got everything done like always. Fast, professional and in a systematic way. Everything lived in my head. The first three years of running my business were intense, hectic and definitely not ones I want to live through ever again.

When I met one of my now collaborative business partners, Francesca Moi (also now known as my sister from another mother and father), she had not yet been in business for 12 months. We hit it off straight away. The very first night we met we decided we would write a book together, and eight months later we wrote *Bums on Seats*. Before that book, she came and did my program and wrote her first book *Follow Me*. Francesca already had a VA and nowadays I think she has three on her team. She was very experienced in seeking them out and knowing how to figure out if they would work out or not. So being close to her, she decided to help me find one. She couldn't believe after six years in business I did not have one.

A few months later, Francesca connected me with Lendy, whom she had recently interviewed. All she said was that Lendy had no experience, but was super smart and willing to learn. We organised a Skype chat so I could meet her and after a 30-minute chat, I decided to hire her. She literally started four hours later. The only system I had written was how to input contact details, names and emails into my database. I had such a backlog of lists to be entered, this kept her busy for almost two weeks! This also allowed me to get to work and write more systems so I could keep her working. Now, four years later, I am so grateful I met her, gave her a go and persisted to make it work for both of us. How I wish I had done it sooner though!!!

Don't delay getting a VA – having one will enable you to focus on the two things that keeps your business alive: sales and marketing. Getting bogged down by admin and repetitive tasks others can complete or hiding behind your computer doing things that won't move your business forward is a complete waste of your precious time. As you grow your business, get yourself to the point where you are only doing the things you love and outsource the rest.

Working with others and having them within your business creates a team environment that is helpful in generating new ideas and problem solving.

As Henry Ford said: 'Coming together is the beginning, staying together is progress and working together is success.'

Introduction

Lendy Macario

Long before I was hired as a virtual assistant, I was a corporate employee. I worked in a finance department for 10 years and spent more than a year in an international non-government organisation before I took up law studies. In December 2015, just after my first bar examinations (which I flunked unfortunately), home-based jobs were becoming popular, but were mostly taken up by 'techy' people. The virtual job that was well-known and accessible at the time was ESL tutorials, so my classmates and I applied. Despite completing a series of trainings, complying to the required internet speed and getting ourselves headsets, we were unsuccessful in winning this type of job.

So, what is a virtual job? It is work performed from the comfort of your home rather than in a physical office provided by an employer. The workload is forwarded to a virtual employee online, via email, direct messages or video calls. At the onset of these home-based positions, the name 'virtual assistant' was established, as the work was originally strictly that of an online assistant or administrator. Now, as the position continues to evolve, a virtual assistant is often called a 'freelancer' because of the wider range of tasks they can manage.

In January 2016, a classmate of mine happened to have a friend who had been working as a virtual assistant for years – and yes, their employer was hiring! I agreed to apply for the virtual assistant job although I didn't have any idea what it would be like. At that time, all I had to offer was the most basic computer and internet knowledge and of course my dedication.

I was scheduled for an interview with an Aussie-based entrepreneur, Francesca Moi – the well-known MeetUp Queen, together with her Philippine based senior VA, Morena. I was very honest. I told them I didn't have a wide knowledge of internet utilisation, social media platforms, websites and other applications, but I am a fast learner and like to take initiative. Boom, right away! They endorsed me to my first and only Boss, NATASA DENMAN! The interview with my Boss was in the morning and by the afternoon I was hired and onboarded. Phheeww, that was too quick! No paper requirements, no qualifications, she just hired me!

So, why did I want to be a VA? Just to get a job, to earn money for myself and my dependents. That was the only motivation I had at the start. But when I landed this job, it felt different from the beginning – like I was on the other side of the world with a new family. I think this job was really designed and meant for me.

To begin with, I was clueless what to do as I only had a pretty basic laptop to work with. On top of this, not being very familiar with the Australian accent, I also had some difficulty understanding what my boss was saying. Natasa suggested I record our conversations so I can replay them whenever I needed to. And there began my VA career.

During the first quarter of my first year, the Denmans – Natasa and Stuart, used to call me every other day to give me instructions on what to do. From the most basic tasks up to complicated ones, they were very organised. I studied everything, I did my research and I showed the utmost enthusiasm and dedication towards my job. I always asked questions and sought clarification because I was so afraid to make mistakes. I thought it would be hard, but with them, everything was just so easy. No more fear or worry that I might be doing the wrong thing!

I was allowed to work up to 40 hours per week. We were using the platform Upwork to monitor my working hours and as the medium for my salary payment. Eventually, the trust was built, and we didn't need the time monitoring app anymore. These days, I just record the number of hours I have worked and send the bill.

I was amazed at how the Denmans ran their business. They have a system which they continue to enhance. I have learnt how to confidently manage several applications, programs and systems. I have also discovered that being a VA can be a lot better than many non-virtual jobs. During my first year, I had this very crucial challenge – I was going to sit the bar exams again. In November 2016, I asked permission to temporarily cut my working hours because I was taking the bar exams. In God's will, I successfully passed this time. The

Boss was very proud, of course. When I passed the bar, it never crossed my mind that I would give up my VA job. I love the job very much and it has helped me big time, financially and in so many ways, so I intend to keep it indefinitely. The working bond between us is strong and the Denmans treat me as family. I feel truly blessed!

CHAPTER 1

SKILLS

What employers look for &
What VAs need to secure the job

What employers look for

Like all business owners, you have a desire to run a successful business with the best team out there. You want everyone to deliver a consistent quality of service and execution of the business systems to your clients and suppliers. When embarking on the search for a VA (and for VAs searching for employment) the following criteria are essential to consider:

- Trust around financials – getting paid, hours worked, credit card security

- Trust around intellectual property and account login details
- Great communication skills in the local language of the business
- Time zone suitability
- Responsiveness
- Stable and fast online connectivity
- Willingness to learn new online platforms
- Organisational skills
- Problem solving abilities and resourcefulness
- Respectful to the team and clients
- Likely duration of employment
- Handover plan in place should employment cease.

Let's break these down with a deeper explanation of what they mean.

Trust around financials

When hiring someone virtually, you cannot see them, feel them or talk to them in the same way you do with people that are physically in your business. You must put a lot of trust into the fact that they are working remotely and doing the right thing. There are ways to protect yourself as you get to know your VA when it comes to financials, but in time you can build up trust and a relationship and work directly just with them. During Lendy's first 12 months of employment we used the freelancing platform that I hired her from as a place where she logged in all her hours and requested her pay on a weekly basis.

As a fee for the service, this platform took 20% of her wages paid by me. Once we got to know each other better and developed trust, I removed her from the platform and started getting her to send me money requests via PayPal on a weekly basis. This gave her an instant 20% pay rise without me being anything more out of pocket. We have now stuck to this system for three years. I am sure she notes down her hours somewhere and can provide them should I ask, but I don't worry about that much. As long as the work I give her is done in a timely manner and she is doing what has been asked of her, I don't micromanage her hours.

From time to time, I do ask her how she spends her time, so that I can see if I want her to stop doing something and do more of other things, but other than that, she is very independent and plans her time accordingly.

Nowadays, Lendy has access to my credit card details to pay for things we need in the business. I trust her completely.

Trust around intellectual property and account login details

This aspect of the work you do with your VA has to rely on trust. The best way to cover this off is at the interview stage and by including it in your agreement with the VA. If you frame it seriously and explain the importance upfront, you should not have any problems. There are platforms such as 1Password that allow for setting up one single password for everything you have, which you can then easily change should you need to, thus instantly locking out anyone from all your login areas and accounts.

Great communication skills in the local language of the business

Every business relies heavily on the ability to communicate clearly and on point. Therefore, you must ensure that when hiring a VA, their language skills in your local language are top notch. You should be able to tell this from the written communication you have with your potential VA in the early stages of employment. The next best place will be during the video interview process. Look past any accents and listen to their grammar and watch their spelling. There will be minor differences that you may notice that is connected to their culture and the way they have learnt the language, but these things are not really a point of worry. Some VAs do not speak directly to clients, so their ability to communicate is not as high a priority – of course they still need to be able to communicate well with you and your team.

Time zone suitability

This is an important consideration when hiring someone in your business. What time will it be at their end during your normal business hours? It's much better if there isn't too much of a time difference as this can play havoc on people's everyday lives and schedules. That is why in Australia, the best place to get an offshore VA is from the Philippines.

There is only a two-hour time difference and many of their people speak amazing English.

You can also hire a VA in your own country, however, expect that you will need to pay them a significantly higher hourly rate than if they are offshore depending on your country's socioeconomic status.

Responsiveness

One of my highest values is to be fast in getting back to people, clients and enquiries. In our business we work on Inbox Zero each and every day. It is only recently that we started introducing weekend and public holiday boundaries. As responsiveness is so high on my values list, I wanted someone that would be the same way – quick to act, answer emails, respond to requests and clear any backlog of pending work.

In anyone that I hire for my business (employees and suppliers), I look at how fast they communicate with me from the time I reach out to them. This initial contact is crucial. It tells me a lot about a person and how they do business or how they will be when working for me. I allow a reasonable time for a response and beyond that often I don't progress with them – 24–48 hours is the longest I will wait within business hours.

Stable and fast online connectivity

The internet has enabled us to do so many wonderful things we could not before. It has given employment to millions of VAs around the world as well as a laptop lifestyle to so many entrepreneurs. As much as the internet is the way we do most things nowadays, it is not always reliable in some locations, which can be frustrating and time consuming.

When hiring a VA, it is important to check their internet speed and connectivity where they live. Weather and remote locations can affect the internet and you can lose contact and pause business operations if this is the case. The best way to check if someone has good internet is to have a video call chat with them (this requires the most bandwidth) and ask them how close they are to a major city in their country.

If the video call works well without cut outs and they are in a major city or close to one, then this is a good sign. Also, ask the VA about this directly and how they would deal with things should the internet stop working. Do they have an alternative? Where else could they go to get online? What is their Plan B and C? They normally will know all this and put you at ease. Sometimes they can use the internet on their phone as a make-do until their home internet comes back online.

Willingness to learn new online platforms

When hiring a VA, they may already be skilled in some of the platforms you use, while others you will need to provide training on. Technology is rapidly evolving and improving, and you will need to embrace those changes – and so will your VA. Since hiring Lendy four years ago, I have trained her in various online platforms such as Dropbox, Asana,

Slack, Amazon, IngramSpark, Active Campaign, etc. More on these platforms later in the book.

The basic skills that they should have is the ability to use Word, Excel, PowerPoint and email platforms – the rest you can provide training for as you go. Screenshot videos are the best form of training for VAs, as they can follow your instructions easily and watch it more than once if needed. They can pause and really take their time. It is also the fastest way for you to develop awesome systems for your business. Later in the book, I will talk about this more in detail.

Organisational skills

This one is a biggie. After all, you are looking to hire a virtual assistant. They need to be organised and be able to come up with ideas and solutions that can help your business run smoothly. Ask them about the rest of their lives and what does an average day look like for them. What do they like doing outside of work? And what kind of experience have they had assisting others?

When I met Lendy, she had just completed her university degree as a lawyer and was studying to pass the bar. She told me not to worry about all this as she is great at managing her own time. She put me at ease and I've never had to worry about this with her. Whenever she needs time off or something urgent pops up at her end, she communicates with me ahead of time and we don't have any issues. Same thing if she may be out of reception or away for some time.

Problem solving abilities and resourcefulness

This skill comes with time as the VA becomes more confident in working with you and the business. Your job is to encourage them to make some of the decisions that they recognise from previous experiences. When something has been repeated multiple times, a system should come into place and the VA should be able to handle it next time.

Encourage your VA to create systems themselves, as this will be a valuable asset to the business for future employees.

Respectful to the team and clients

It is important to communicate to your VA how you would like them to be around clients, team members and you. Lendy wanted to call me 'Madam' as in her Philippine culture that is how you address your boss. I didn't like that as in our culture it's not a commonly used word and made me feel like I was an old lady. So, together we decided that she calls me 'Boss' as she did not feel comfortable calling me just by my name as you would in our culture. She also calls my husband 'Sir Boss', my mum 'Mum' and then other team members by their name and with clients she uses the title Ms or Mr with their first name. Even though this is not required, I have found that clients like that extra bit of respect being addressed more formally, so I have not mentioned to her to stop. It also fits with her personality and flavour.

Through communicating the business values and who we are as people, we have found a common culture inside our business which resonates our main values of fast, fun, fame and family.

Likely duration of employment

Staff retention is always on an employer's mind. How long will this person stay with us after we invest time and money training them up? It is one of the biggest costs to a business. That is why, when you are hiring a VA, this is something you should ask at the very beginning. How long do you intend on working as a VA? Are you interested in short-term or long-term employment? Tell them what you are looking for and why it is important to you.

For me, I wanted something long term and stable with Lendy. I was worried her law degree will send her in the direction of what she had studied, but she assured me she could handle both. The income she can earn as a VA supersedes the income she can earn practising law in her country so this was an opportunity she did not want to pass up. It has proven to be the case and we are now four years in and going strong.

Lendy is super smart and I always look to give her new tasks and things to do to challenge her. We recently changed her job title from virtual assistant to event coordinator as that is mostly the type of work that she does for me. She is now also taking on a further role of a publications assistant alongside my personal assistant who is more the publications coordinator now.

Handover plan in place should employment cease

The final thing I suggest you discuss with your potential VA from the very beginning is the contingency plan should they want to cease employment with you in the future. I remember asking Lendy if she would spend 2–4 weeks in a handover stage with a new VA if she wanted to go and do something different. We even put this in our employment agreement at the time. Each year when we have a chat about her employment, I confirm that this will still be ok with her should she decide to leave the business. She always reassures me that she will help me to find someone new and do what she can to make sure the handover goes smoothly.

* * *

What VAs need to secure the job

There are so many things to consider when seeking VA jobs. In my situation, I was just so lucky that I was able to get the job even though I was not fully prepared. I had been in the corporate world for 10 years before moving into a home-based one and the work environment was entirely different.

If you're serious about becoming a VA, as a minimum, these are the basic skills you'll need:

- Great written and oral communication skills
- Excellent command of the English language
- Organisational skills, punctuality and work ethics

- Basic computer and internet knowledge (advanced skills are an advantage)
- Social media management, search engine and Microsoft Office Suite savvy
- The confidence to use your initiative and creativity as required
- A high-level of responsiveness and understanding that employers hate waiting.

If you think that you lack some skills and the job requires them, you can always make use of your initiative to search for online tutorials, ask some experts in the field or even enrol in short courses. Remember, your capital is your skills, and you need to be willing to invest in upskilling, as new learnings work to your advantage. Moreover, obtaining great referrals and awesome job reviews/ratings from previous employers is a huge plus.

If you are looking to secure a long-term virtual assistant role, be sure to make this clear with your prospective employer. Usually, employers will target long-term employment relationships, especially in the case of virtual employees, since trust building requires time especially when its online. It is not easy hiring one virtual employee and needing to do the same the following month. It costs time, money and is a huge effort on the part of the employer. So, make sure you are committed to working as a VA for a reasonable period of time.

Finding the right VA position

Today, a huge number of jobs that were previously only offered in a physical office are now also accessible online or home-based. When identifying the right position for you, try asking yourself these questions:

- Which jobs/industries interest you most?
- What skills do you currently have?
- Which time zone best suits your working hours?

If you look at the type of virtual positions available online, you'll find a wide variety of jobs such as administration, social media management, real estate marketing, architecture, accounting, bookkeeping, tutorials, web and graphic design, and many more. Base your job hunting around the existing skills that you have, or those that you can upskill yourself with, to enable you to secure the job that matches your talents.

Preparing yourself for a home-based role

Working from home is actually pretty awesome. You don't need to spend time every morning grooming yourself before starting work, except when you have a meeting or conference scheduled, for which you must look good of course. All you need to prepare and set yourself up to work is a fast internet connection, reliable computer and a cool working space. That's it!

In addition, before you decide to work from home, you'll also need to assess yourself. Can you commit to working alone and virtually? Are you comfortable communicating via your computer, video call conferences, chats, emails, etc.? Are you committed to deliver the output expected of you? Will you be able to effectively balance your work and personal time?

Advantages of home-based jobs

Being a virtual assistant, your job becomes your life, however, you also have the luxury to have time for yourself and family. When you are home-based, you save time from early morning preparation, transportation and idle breaks. You can dedicate this time instead to your personal routines and family errands. Here's a short list of some of the advantages:

- No pressure on early morning personal routines (no bath, no problem)
- No more stressful peak-hour traffic rush to deal with
- More flexibility to do what you want during your breaks
- No need to buy your lunch, you can enjoy healthy home-cooked food
- Save time and money previously spent on transportation going to work
- No annoying or difficult office colleagues sharing your space
- A more organised house as you can multitask with your chores.

With my Ultimate 48 Hour Author family, I manage my time efficiently. I use techniques to speed up my tasks and my working hours are flexible. If I'm not available on a certain day or time, I inform my Boss right away because I know the system well and know how they want things to be done. They always have a set time frame for each task, and I don't want to leave them hanging. Basically, if you care for your job, you will feel uncomfortable if you don't feel you've had an excellent output at the end of the day.

The things that matter and keep you interested in the work

Just like in the corporate world, the things that keep you interested are generally fair compensation, being part of a good company and healthy relationships with your workmates. As a VA for more than four years now, there are so many things that keep me happy and motivated to work harder. These include:

- **Great bosses:** Natasa and Stuart demonstrate the kind of leadership that makes the team grow and are not into micromanagement.
- **Flexible working hours:** Although I start working at seven in the morning, if there are things that I should be attending to at 6am like logistics emails, I manage it, or even beyond 6pm if I can do it. I always treat the business as my own business so if there is something outstanding, if I can, I get it done. Same thing if I have some personal errands to be done within working hours, I inform the team and fit it in.

- **Working in the comfort of my own home:** For all the reasons mentioned above! Saves me time and money and avoids the stress of corporate life.
- **Good salary:** The Boss always assesses my wage every year and if appropriate will give me a salary increase. Thumbs up to her that she does this – I have already had three salary increases in just four years working with the team.
- **Well-established system and workflow:** The systems in place are tried, tested and revised as needed, which makes my workday run smoothly and more efficiently.
- **Beautiful and very professional teammates:** Working with great people keeps me motivated and I always feel supported and valued as a member of the team.
- **Awesome work dynamics:** From a virtual assistant to event coordinator, I have gained so much knowledge about publishing, mentoring and social media exposure techniques.

What kind of boss do VAs hope for?

When I was still a college student, I used to wish that I could work with an AWESOME BOSS. I didn't meet that kind of boss until I became a VA. I now think I have the best boss ever!

Generally, VAs hope for the kind of boss who can manage people effectively. Having an efficient employee is a result of good leadership. My boss is very calm, organised and systematic, so everything is in order. If things go wrong, the

Boss doesn't panic at all, instead, she has a lot of options to manage every problem and rectify it. She is never bossy and always sets a great example for us.

As an employee, we also hope that our boss will be appreciative, positive, happy and funny – not a grimacing old maid (lol), because it is always best to work with someone who is always in a good mood.

OVER TO YOU:

1. Document the skills you are looking for before starting your search for a VA.

2. Write down all the tasks in your business you believe you can outsource.

3. If you are wanting to be a VA – list all the skills and competencies you can bring to the table and how they relate to some of the things we have discussed in this chapter.

CHAPTER 2

FIND

Where to find a VA & Where to look for work as a VA

Where to find a VA

When it comes to my business, I'm frequently asked where I found my VA – which is why this topic deserves its own chapter! There are three ways to seek out a VA: via freelancing websites, through VA agencies or by word of mouth. In this chapter I will cover off the pros and cons of each as well as the important things you must know, so that you can find the right method for you.

Hiring via a freelancing website or word of mouth

I actually found Lendy through word of mouth. Francesca's VA had a friend who was looking for work and she interviewed her thinking she may hire her for her business but ended up recommending her to me. However, after I interviewed Lendy on Skype, we set up an account on Upwork and used that freelancing website for the first 12 months as a way to pay her, manage her hours and keep it all safe and secure until we built up more trust between one another.

There are thousands of VAs looking for work on Upwork from all over the world. At the time of writing this book, it is the most popular freelancing website out there. I have hired many experts via Upwork and continue to do so. Other commonly used websites for VAs are Guru, VA Networking and Hubstaff Talent.

Let's look at the pros and cons of using a freelancing website or word of mouth to find a VA.

PROS:
- Dealing directly with the person you will be working with
- They may have limited experience, but you can work this out by interviewing them
- Expect to pay almost half of the hourly rate compared to an agency VA per hour
- You can easily search for VAs worldwide
- Secure payment system where you can track hours and pay on completion of work.

CONS:
- There is no insurance behind getting someone that is dodgy – the risk is higher
- Your VA can disappear and leave you in the lurch without a replacement
- VAs looking for work on freelancing websites are not formally trained as a VA.

Hiring through a VA agency

Now let's turn our attention to hiring a VA via an agency:

PROS:
- More professional
- They provide training to their VAs, so you are likely to get someone more experienced
- If your VA is sick, you are likely to get a replacement
- If your VA chooses to leave your employment, they will find you a replacement instantly
- Secure way to deal with VAs
- You don't need to interview them
- Easy way to grow and scale your business by hiring more VAs as you need them.

CONS:
- Only one, but a big one for new small business owners tight on cashflow – the hiring rate is a lot higher than finding someone privately. After all, you are paying the VA as well as the company providing them. You are also paying for the training they provide, spotters fees and ongoing support.

Additional benefits of word of mouth

As mentioned above, the pros and cons of finding someone through word of mouth are similar to those of hiring via a freelance agency, however there is less risk is involved. You are getting a recommendation from someone that you (hopefully) know and trust, so the risk of a bad experience is lower. I often get asked if I know any other VAs that are looking for work from my authors, or Lendy sometimes asks me if I have any authors looking for VAs. From time to time those around her decide they would like to do what she does and then we end up connecting them with our clients. This is a safer way to find the right match as there is a personal connection.

Of course, Lendy would not want to recommend someone that won't do a good job or that she doesn't know well. This is also part of the reason we decided to write this book. I wanted to empower small business owners to take the leap into hiring a VA earlier rather than later in their business and I wanted to find a way for Lendy to generate extra income for recommending VAs that want to do what she does. We don't have a goal to be an agency as we already operate a business we love. In a way, we want to become connectors of people, who then allow them to develop their work relationships independently beyond the introduction.

Our intention is to pick the best of both worlds, by blending the safety of someone known being introduced and keeping it more affordable for the business owner long term. I know my authors want that type of solution and have often asked this of me.

✳ ✳ ✳

Where to look for work as a VA

As a beginner, I highly recommend creating an account on freelancing websites such as Upwork, OnlineJobs.ph, Toptal, Guru, etc., so you can build your profile as a freelancer/VA. These websites also provide a platform to manage payments and hours. When I started out as a VA, I created an account on Upwork and the Boss and I managed my hours and salary through the platform, which worked well for us for the first year.

Within platforms like Upwork, you can customise your profile to reflect your capabilities and level of skills. This is important, as when you apply for jobs, this is what can set you apart from the other applicants. Take the time to complete your profile, because when your profile is rated 100%, you are more likely to receive invitations to interview from prospective employers.

There are many advantages of finding VA work via a freelancing website, including:

- Access to millions of jobs
- Easy to send job proposals to clients
- Free trainings, examinations, tutorials, assistance
- Guaranteed salary on hours worked
- Safe payment facility
- Tools to record your working hours.

The cons of working through a freelancer website, mainly relate to fees and holding period of your wages:

- A service fee is deducted from your wage, which can be up to 20%
- Your funds are not released into your bank account immediately, there is a holding period of 2–4 days.

Word of mouth is a great way to connect with potential employers, so if you are interested in securing a VA position, be sure to put the word out to friends, family, co-workers or classmates. You never know who may know someone who is looking for a VA!

There is also the option of registering with an agency. This is not something I've personally had experience with, but it is worth exploring if you prefer to have the backing of an agency or are unable to source work independently. It can also be a good option if you have specialised skills or experience, as employers who are looking for a VA with a certain level of expertise (and are willing to pay more to find it) will often approach an agency rather than search for a freelancer independently.

Want to take things to the next level? In the Philippines, a group of freelancers did just that, building a freelancing empire in 2017. They organise conferences, webinars and tutorials on how to become successful virtual employees and train people with the skills the online world needs such as graphic and web design, Shopify and Amazon skills, data entry, administrative expertise, cold calling, Facebook, Instagram advertising and more. They have helped many people get started as a VA and built a successful business for themselves in the process.

How can you advertise yourself?

Selling yourself as a VA, is actually quite similar to applying for a job in a big-time company. You present your skills, availability, rate and personality. For example, if a graphic designer is applying for a position, they'll provide a portfolio with sample designs, possibly create some designs for the prospective employer and include other relevant information in their proposal such as existing skills, previous experience, availability and hourly rate.

I was once approached by someone who was looking for guidance on how to be a VA. I was already into my second year as a VA when he decided to resign from his work as a call centre agent, so I suggested he create an account with Upwork and start promoting himself. After a month of job hunting via Upwork, he landed a job, and within the year he created his own virtual assistant business where he hires VAs for prospective employers. In the space of just a few short years, he has built a successful and meaningful business within the VA industry and is now loving his working life.

Some innovative freelancers even create advertisements and promotions via social media to attract high-end employers. If you'd like to advertise on social platforms, here are some catchy VA taglines you could try:

- Hire a virtual assistant today and grow your business tomorrow.

- Exhausted? No time for yourself or your family? Hire me and I will make your life and business easier!
- Find out what a VA can do for you and your business.

You can also use Canva to create nice images to go with your taglines to catch people's attention.

✳ ✳ ✳

OVER TO YOU:

1. Join upwork.com and look at some VA profiles or contact a few agencies to discuss your requirements.

2. Complete interviews with the potential VAs on your shortlist

3. If you are wanting to be a VA – put your profile up on upwork.com and start promoting yourself on social media by creating catchy images on Canva.

CHAPTER 3

MONEY

Paying your VA &
Setting your rate as a VA and
asking for a pay rise

Paying your VA

One of the first questions I asked Francesca (who helped me find Lendy) was to understand how much to pay her. What is fair and reasonable for the work she will be doing, taking into consideration the average pay of VAs in the Philippines? As Lendy had no experience as a VA, we started on a lower hourly rate for her until she had completed her first month of work and then went up from there to reach her regular rate.

Over the years, I have given her pay rises as she has become a more experienced and valuable team member taking on more responsibility.

Important things to look at when deciding how much you are willing to pay your VA are:

- Where do they live and what is that country's socioeconomic status?
- What are other VAs earning per hour in that country on average?
- What currency does the VA expect to be paid in – a lot of the time this is USD which can affect the rate depending on how your currency is fairing. Lately, the Australian dollar has significantly dropped against the US dollar, so it is costing our business a lot more to pay our VA and suppliers we pay in USD.
- How experienced is the VA? With less experience, the rate should be lower until they get trained up more.
- What have they earned in the past? If you can find this out by asking about previous employment it may give you a guideline of what to offer them.
- Will you be giving your VA other bonuses and incentives?

Once you make your offer and they accept it, draft up an agreement. I wrote the agreement with Lendy myself, as it made her employment more official. The reason I didn't engage a lawyer is because if anything happened, our Australian agreements do not have jurisdiction in another country, so spending money on a lawyer for a written agreement would have been a waste of time.

This is another reason why those that want to take on less risk, hire their VA from a VA agency as described in the previous chapter and stay protected along the way. Usually the agreement will be with the VA agency that is based in your local country and therefore if anything did happen, you would be able to lodge a legal dispute.

The main reason I drafted up an agreement with Lendy (even though it didn't have any official legal standing), was to illustrate that I was taking this seriously and so was she. Sometimes, the sheer fact you sign something and do a handshake can be enough for people of integrity and loyalty to do the right thing.

Here is a copy of our agreement when we began this journey four years ago:

Agreement for Virtual Assistant Work

Date: 18 January 2016
Company: Ultimate 48 Hour Author
Owners: Natasa Denman and Stuart Denman
Employee: Lendy Castillo Macario

Term: Part time with view to work full time in the future
Training period: 1 month with payment of $ X USD per hour
After training month: $ X USD per hour

Terms and Conditions:

1. Natasa and Stuart will provide the systems, passwords and training to assist with their administrative and digital tasks.

2. Lendy with complete work in a timely manner as communicated and document time on a Time Log spreadsheet.

3. At the end of each week we will release payment for the hours worked at the stated rate. Training time is also included in working hours.

4. At the completion of tasks, Lendy will advise Natasa or Stuart so that the work can be checked and confirmed as complete.

5. We will use Facebook to communicate quicker.

6. We will have a weekly meeting to discuss the tasks to be completed that week.

7. Lendy will communicate ahead of time, minimum 2 days' notice if she cannot work on a certain day.

8. On odd occasions we may request something over the weekend.

9. We will complete the hiring procedure via Upwork. com once Lendy's profile has been reviewed and release payment via there.

10. If Lendy is to terminate this agreement, she is to give 4 weeks' notice during which time she will help out to find a replacement and train them to the company's standards and expectations.

We look forward to having you as part of our team and together doing lots of fun and productive work.

Space for Signatures here...

As you can see it was fairly short, simple and to the point. We have never needed anything else. Could Lendy have broken the terms of this agreement? Absolutely. I was willing to take the risk on her and her on us and with time we developed a strong work and personal relationship. We now have an obligation to one another to do the right thing and take care of each other. This is called doing the right thing for those you care about. It does become a lot more than just employer and employee after a while.

Making payments to your VA and pay rises

I mentioned previously that for the first year, we used the Upwork platform to release payments to Lendy on a weekly basis as protection to myself and the business. However, once trust was earned a great way I could give her a 20% pay rise without paying anything extra out of my own pocket, was to take her off Upwork and pay directly into her PayPal account. This has worked like magic since then. Lendy logs her hours, sends me a money request and I release the payment as soon as I get her request from PayPal. There really isn't too much to it.

When is the right time to give your VA a pay rise? For me, it is after the first training month when I can see they are doing things on their own without much assistance, and/ or when they take on new responsibilities and tasks. From there, I suggest an annual review as they remain loyal and become a long-standing member of your team.

Bonuses and incentives

From time to time, you may feel your VA has been consistently putting in a great effort and really supporting you in running your business. Consider surprising them with the occasional bonus. For VAs living in the more disadvantaged countries, this counts for a lot and they really appreciate it. Times that a bonus may come in handy or as a nice surprise would be on their birthday, as a Christmas bonus, if they are going through some tough times at home or if your business has had an amazing sales period and is doing well. I love to reward everyone for the hard work they have put in and I prefer to just surprise them rather than promise bonuses.

When it comes to incentives, this works a bit different. If your VA is interested in making some extra cash, how can you create some activities and outcomes that they need to be responsible for that can earn them those incentives? Here is an example of what we have set up. Lendy has full access to my social media channels and she can post on my behalf in groups and promote our events and products. As this is going to propel the business forward financially, we decided it was fair to give her a percentage or dollar amount of each of the sales that are generated as a result of her promotions. Sales are the hardest thing to generate in a business and it's also the bloodline of any sustainable and successful business, so the more people you have doing it in the business the better it is for everyone.

We have similar incentives set up with my publications coordinator who works alongside me. Make sure you do pay out what you have promised in a timely manner and get them to take the responsibility on reporting and documenting what has been done and how, so it can be repeated in the future.

This year in our business, the theme is 'Sales'. Everyone on the team will be taking a course in sales and we'll also be doing further training for the team as a whole. This will help everyone make more money in addition to their standard wage. Every year we have a different theme and focus on getting better at that. For example, last year was all about 'Publishing' as we launched our in-house publishing company ·Ultimate World Publishing, we needed to master the steps, create the systems and get the publishing machine operating at an optimum level. What will be your theme this year?

Trips to your VA and them visiting you

After a certain period of time, you may start to feel like you know your VA really well, but you have never met them face to face. At this point, it may be a good idea to make the effort to meet them in real life. For us this happened after three and a half years, by which time the team had grown to include not just my VA, but also my mum and my personal assistant. I made a decision to invest in a work conference we could hold in the Philippines for the four of us. My husband had to stay behind with the kids, but in a couple of years we may take everyone along.

I booked a beautiful villa on the island of Boracay in the Philippines and we spent eight amazing days there. Getting to know each other in a different way, planning, discussing and celebrating the year that we had. I believe this was a tremendously valuable investment in the team and business. Meeting Lendy for the first time did not feel strange. It was as if we had known each other for years – which we had but only virtually. She was also able to get to know, Viv, my personal assistant with whom they work together and catch up on a weekly basis for an update and planning meeting.

On this trip we also decided this was going to now become an annual event and that next year we would go on a cruise and get Lendy to Australia so that she can experience where the business is run and attend some of our events and retreat in real life. She has watched everything from the other side of the computer and the time has come to have her here with us. We are going to host her at our place for the month and in this time a lot of other valuable work and planning will happen. She will also understand what we do and how we do it much better.

Taking a trip out to visit your VA or getting them to come to you can really benefit your business long term. With these types of incentives, you will also improve your staff retention rate and team morale. If your team is having fun, feeling fulfilled and appreciated working for you, why would they want to leave?

Cultural differences around money

In some cultures, it's considered impolite to ask for money or pay rises. Be sure to understand this if you have a VA from one of those cultures. Do the right thing, conduct regular reviews and discuss this openly with them. They can be very loyal and simply too respectful to bring up the subject. You are the leader, so act like it and don't avoid the subject. In some of the disadvantaged countries your VA may be supporting a family of 5–10 people with their income.

* * *

Setting your rate as a VA and asking for a pay rise

Bringing up the subject of a pay rise is not a problem with me being the VA of the Denmans. The Boss has this system of assessing things regularly to see if I am entitled to a pay rise or not. So far, I've never needed to request a pay rise since the Boss is acting on it without me asking. One time she did ask about rates of VAs around me and so I was honest to tell her, this is the current rate here in the Philippines and so on. For me, it would be very awkward to ask for a pay rise especially because my work before has been incredibly easy, very flexible and comfortable.

So, how can you ask for a pay rise when the circumstances demand? My advice would be to write a letter to your boss and lay out everything. This includes your current rate, the current rates of other VAs with similar tasks, the work difficulties, the effort that you are exerting and so on, to explain the need for a pay rise. It is not weird to ask for a pay rise if you really deserve it. Most bosses will surely understand and give you a raise once they see fit – we just sometimes need to remind them since they have plenty of things on their mind, so be sure to ask politely.

In November 2019, two of my VA friends told me they had two weeks of leave with pay coming up in December and they were very excited. They asked me if I have that vacation leave with pay, too since I am a more senior VA than them and so I replied maybe my Boss is already planning it or maybe I will ask during our trip to New Zealand and Australia. I did not ask when my friends told me about the news because I know even without asking that my Boss may award me more than that. If you sense that it won't really happen because maybe your boss is extremely busy, you may care to ask courteously. There's no harm in asking.

Payment methods – Upwork vs. PayPal

For the first timer, being paid via Upwork is kind of a disadvantage because you will be charged 20% in fees from your total pay. However, once you reach a certain amount of payments from that employer (currently $500), the deduction is reduced to 10%, and if you reach the $10,000 billed salary mark, the deduction is reduced to 5%. Another disadvantage is that you must wait for 2–4 days before your money is available in your bank accounts. So, for example, if the payment is approved on Monday, the amount will be available in your bank sometime between Wednesday and Friday.

Aside from the deduction and delay, there are lots of advantages to using Upwork as your payment platform, such as:

- Your salary is safe and guaranteed
- You'll get a higher dollar exchange rate

- There are bonuses and award programs
- There is a membership status appraisal
- You get ratings and reviews from employers
- You can access online trainings to improve your profile
- It's easy to use the time logging to track your hours.

Upwork is really designed for virtual assistants and freelancers. Opportunities are being posted there every minute and freelancers can apply and send proposals to prospective employers quickly and easily in their own time.

As for PayPal, it is mainly just used as a payment platform for transfer of funds. The deduction rate is about 5% and the dollar conversion is lower than Upwork. Upwork has so much more to offer to freelancers but it takes time and effort to get approved as a member, and you must build your profile as unique from other freelancers, otherwise, you will be rejected. So, if you want to work for lots of clients, join Upwork – but if you are loyal with only one employer, use PayPal for convenience.

Bonuses and real-life meetups

Every now and then, Boss surprises me with bonuses. This is usually in December but sometimes she does it unexpectedly. I often get emails that I received cash from Natasa Denman with a special note such as, 'get some pretty dresses or stuff that you like for this Christmas'. It is indeed heartwarming, and I feel so blessed.

Last year, some of my VA friends went to Australia to meet their Boss and stayed there for a month. I was like...wow! They did it! One VA friend asked me when I will be going to Australia and I said maybe I am not ready yet. But of course, surprises strike anytime. I never imagined that my Boss and her mum plus our publications coordinator Viv would visit me in the Philippines. The virtual bubble has been pierced since I met them in person, finally!

The team treated me so well and we stayed in Boracay (one of the most famous beaches in the world) for eight days. It was awesome! My virtual work is now more connected and real since we worked together in Boracay. But wait, there was another shocking surprise that Boss announced while travelling to the Philippines – we are going to go on a cruise to New Zealand and I am going to visit Australia in 2020! OMG! I was certainly stunned as tickets to the cruise were already booked and I have the confirmation! I had a pinch myself moment then.

How does a VA income compare?

Working as a VA has really helped me a lot especially when I was still reviewing for the bar exams. When I started as a VA, I was supporting my brother's education and myself. If I compare my virtual job income to a corporate job income here in the Philippines, my salary is way beyond. Why? If I earn P30,000.00 as a VA, I earn it in full – but, when I earn P30,000.00 as a regular employee in a company here, I might be actually earning P15,000.00 net because I have more expenses such as transportation, meals, uniforms, make-up and other daily costs. Overall, this makes a huge difference.

At this point of time, since I am not so far into full practice of my profession being a lawyer, I am not earning much. I don't have litigation clients (paying clients) but I have my notarial practice. So, to compare, my VA job is still my main source of income. My brother has also graduated from college, thanks to my VA job!

* * *

OVER TO YOU:

1. Write up a basic agreement between you and your VA.

2. Decide on what you are willing to pay per hour for your VA at the training stage and beyond. Be sure you are able to clearly explain what the future may look like in your business.

3. As a VA working from home, list out all the other expenses you won't have over working in a different job.

CHAPTER 4

TOOLS

Essential online tools your business needs & Tips to help you learn and master new programs

---

Essential online tools your business needs

With the huge leaps in technology that have happened over the past couple of decades, working online has become easier and easier. Not only are VAs working online, but a lot of business owners are choosing businesses that provide them with the laptop lifestyle away from a bricks and mortar business. In order to run your business online successfully and efficiently you must spend a bit of time in the set up and learning of the tools that will make your life easy and your business super organised. In this chapter we will go into detail on some of the core tools that you need to be using with your VA so they can do their job with ease.

Here are the main programs we use on a daily basis:

- Word, Excel and PowerPoint
- Outlook for emails
- YouTube for video content uploading and sharing
- Dropbox for file sharing and storage
- Active Campaign for database management
- Zoom for team and client meetings
- Slack for team and supplier communication
- Asana for project management
- Facebook for client interaction, community building, adding value and promotions.

I will go into more detail on these and how we use them, so you can gain an understanding of what the best set up is for you. Over time these platforms may change and become unavailable, but I strongly encourage you to look for something similar that can be used to execute the same tasks.

Word, Excel and PowerPoint

The Microsoft Office suite should be a staple for any business. It's recognised and used worldwide for word processing, spreadsheets and presentation building. Most people you meet nowadays know how to use them and at a very minimum when you engage a VA, they should know how to operate the Microsoft Office suite. If they don't know these programs, I would not hire them. This is how we use them when working with Lendy:

- In **Word** we create a lot of template text for various things that she can copy and paste as responses to clients. We deal only with Word files when working with our clients. Be mindful, those that use Mac computers may have Pages (which is the alternative to Word), but editors and most others do not edit work in Pages. It is always best even if you have a Mac computer (as all my technology is Apple) that you install Microsoft Office onto it and work with what is commonly used across the board.

- **Excel** is used a lot in our business, as we do a lot of events and are constantly working with lists of people coming to events or retreats and we document that data into spreadsheets. Having rows and columns allows you to organise the information better and the ability to add new sheets on the same files means you can expand and organise your work in one place. I love seeing some of the stuff Lendy comes up with using Excel to make things so clear at a glance.

- **PowerPoint** is used for the creation of our presentations. I am the one that works with it mostly as I design and write them, however I do know a lot of other business owners who write the content and then just give it to their VA to input into a beautiful design for their presentation with their branding. My husband hates doing presentation slides as he is not very visual, so I am always helping him. A VA should be able to assist with this easily if you provide a bit of training and communication of what you want.

Investment: Microsoft Office will set you back a monthly subscription fee or annual fee whichever way you decide to pay it. It's no longer advisable to download the program on your computer and have access indefinitely as you'll miss out on valuable features and functions. By paying a monthly fee, you get access to all the updates and upgrades they do over time so that you are always working on the latest and best version. The fees vary depending on how many licenses you need to buy in the business. Look it up or ask an IT Expert to work out exactly what you need. Once you buy your license, your VA should also be able to install it at their end with the login details as the program download is accessed online.

Email management

Email is one of the most important things to get right. It's something that most small business owners struggle with and get overwhelmed by. That is one area your VA will be able to help you with immensely. I want to share some tips with you on email as I believe we have it sorted and have conquered the information overload that hits our inboxes every day, but I will do that a bit later on. For now, let's just discuss the system you may be using and how you should have it set up.

We use Microsoft Outlook as our program to manage our emails. There are many other systems that work in a similar way. The most important thing is to have things set up correctly. Something I didn't realise until I engaged an IT expert for help was the fact that not having things set up correctly can mean my emails may not get through. I also had to clear my emails on each of my devices. Another thing that used to happen was that each time I travelled internationally, I could not reply or send emails from my accounts as they were not connected properly with the outgoing server. I was always having to resort to my Yahoo email when travelling. This was really annoying as that email I only use for personal stuff and don't want business enquiries coming to it.

When my IT expert told me all the reasons I was having all this trouble, I decided to get him to help me set everything up properly. A few days later, everything was connected. My VA saw the emails I did, she could delete and respond and then those emails would magically disappear at my end. When I travelled everything worked as it does back home. So much time and frustration saved. I felt free and much better organised. Nowadays when an email hits our inbox, myself, my husband, Lendy and my PA see it. Most of us can handle most emails and some are relevant to specific people depending on the request that has come in. Whoever sees it can file it away for the person that needs to address it and keep the inbox clear every single day. The pending inboxes get cleared all business days so there really isn't anything sitting in there for too long. If someone is on holidays, others pick up their stuff and nothing ever gets missed.

We also have other folders and subfolders that we file away important emails for safekeeping. These are things like emailed agreements, email sign offs for other things from clients, template emails, electronic invoices/receipts and anything that is a major category where you need to store away emails for future reference. Everything else gets deleted and these folders are reviewed every 3–6 months and are decluttered of emails that are no longer relevant. Here is a look inside our Outlook inbox:

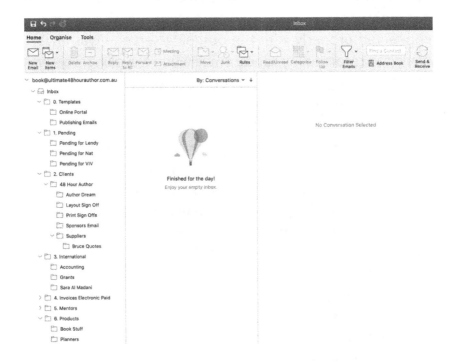

Most business owners dream of an inbox like this and often ask how we are so on top of everything all the time. Consistency would be my one-word answer! But let me give you my top 10 practical tips to get on top of your inbox and finally feel free of the overwhelm email can create. I suggest you also teach these tips to your VA and the rest of the team.

1. Keep your email accounts to a minimum – think of your business inbox as the reception desk where everything comes in and can then get filed away for the specific person in a pending folder. In our business, myself and my husband have our personal branding emails and then one single business email (which makes a total of three) for the whole team. Our VA and PA do not have their own accounts. They still just work through the three, however it is the business one they reply from with their personal signature at the bottom, so clients know who has responded.

2. Have one email account for the junk, such as any memberships you get, or anything you opt in to receive. Whenever you get asked for an email account by another business, only give out that account. For me that is my Yahoo account, which I call my personal account for my life stuff. I do give my business email for things that are business related that need to come there so I can file them away in my folders. The good thing about picking an account like Yahoo, Gmail, Hotmail or the like, is that you can use an app called Unroll.Me and unsubscribe quickly and easily from companies you no longer want to hear from. You cannot set up Unroll.Me on other email accounts that go through a private server. I unsubscribe on Unroll.Me every three months and this keeps the influx of emails at a minimum as I only hear from the companies that I want to.

3. If you are currently sitting at 9878 or 99786 emails in your inbox, press the delete button on all of them. I see these kinds of numbers so frequently on my clients' phones and computers that it makes me cringe. I don't even know how they have space to think. I am the kind of person that does not have a single notification on the phone and clears things 2–3 times a day consistently, so I have time for everything in my life. If you have that many emails, you will never go through them. If you delete something important and if that person really needs you, they will email again or try to phone you. Either delete it all and start fresh or go through emails that came in the last 7-10 days, take care of them and then hit delete on the rest. You will feel amazing!!!

4. Create folders and file things you need to keep so they don't live in your inbox. Basically, nothing should live in your inbox. Don't file everything – only super important stuff like I mentioned earlier. To give you an idea, 80% of my emails get deleted immediately, 15% need to be answered and actioned and 5% get stored or filed away, if not less.

5. Unsubscribe from other businesses regularly. You can always subscribe again if you need to hear from them.

6. Set up your system so that your whole team picks up all the emails that come in. If something needs

to be super private, then encourage a phone call with the client. Always let your clients know that the whole team will see their email, so they don't write anything private they don't want anyone else to know.

7. Keep clients away from Facebook Messenger and all questions and enquiries are to come to email – more on this in the Facebook section.

8. Put up an Out of Office auto reply during weekends (we do between 5:30pm Friday and 8am Monday) and at times you are away for an extended period of time, to let those that email you know how and when you will respond. This also allows you to communicate boundaries and not get bombarded with emails. When we did this, it made everything so much easier and more organised. You can train your clients how to treat you by communicating exactly how things will be.

Here are two examples of our out of office emails we have set up for weekends and the Christmas break that you can rewrite and use for yourself:

Weekend out of office:

Hey there,

Hope the weekend has started amazing for you. The Ultimate 48 Hour Author team are also taking a breather until 9am Monday Melbourne time. If there is anything urgent that cannot wait until then please text Natasa on XXXX XXX XXX or Stuart on XXXX XXX XXX, otherwise your email will be responded to on Monday.

Warm regards,
Natasa, Stuart and the U48A Team xxx

Christmas break out of office:

Hey there,

PLEASE READ FULLY IF YOU HAVE NOT READ IT BEFORE...
Thanks so much for your email. You will receive this out of office reply from 1 Dec to 15 Jan each time you email us, as you may not have seen or read the below info on our movements during this period.

The team at Ultimate 48 Hour Author and Ultimate World Publishing pride themselves on being able to respond to all communication in a swift manner to keep all your projects moving along as fast as possible. We are always on top of all questions and requests during business hours and work on inbox zero. As we move into the quieter part of the year and the festive season, please note the following:

- We will only respond to emails during normal business hours especially during December and January. You may have noticed that we have set up a regular out of office email on weekends alerting you to this.

- Please don't send questions or enquiries on Facebook Messenger – use email as the platform to communicate regarding the project we are working on. Facebook is ok to share fun stuff, things you want to celebrate and to ask questions in the secret group as a forum. You will get a faster answer on email than Facebook anytime as one of the four of us will pick it up rather the single person you may have messaged.

- The Denman Family and Viv will be in a different time zone from 8 Dec to 4 Jan – we are heading to Utah for a White Xmas and Viv is visiting her mum and sister in the UK. Note this in terms of the delay in email responses you may experience when we are in these time zones.

- During the trips away, as family time will be prioritised, we will only check and respond to communication once a day on business days to keep everything ticking along.

- Note that just because we are available and will respond to you during normal business hours, some of our editors, designers and the printers will generally shut down 20 Dec to 6 Jan. This would mean, we have sent your work across but we are waiting for them to come back to business.

All of these initiatives are now in place as we work towards improving quality of life and quantity of focused time with our loved ones. I recently read a book called *Indistractable* by Nil Eyal where I picked up some awesome further tips and strategies on how to be focused on the things that are really important in our lives – self, family and work. Check it out – it's an easy read and really puts things in perspective. It may change how you approach 2020.

We wish every single one of you a wonderful festive season, quality time with your families and we can't wait to smash a wonderful 2020 after a much-needed time to rest, recharge and reflect on the year that it has been.

Lots of Love, Nat, Stu, Viv & Lendy xxxx

9. Schedule your responses to clients – if you are anything like me, you like to answer what comes in immediately and be done with it. However, what this does is that it starts the email ping pong whereby an enquiry may need a few back and forward replies to get to the end of it. Instead, if it's the weekend and you are really wanting to clear your inbox, answer the email however schedule the reply to go out 8am Monday morning. This reply will then sit in your drafts till Monday morning and you can delete the incoming email and have a clear inbox. Your client will get a response during business hours as promised and you won't be overwhelmed on a Monday to answer 100s of emails. Train your VA to do the same so that how the team responds is consistent. Enjoy the rest of your weekend and in time, less and less emails will come to you out of business hours.

10. Train your whole team on these tips. Everyone must operate the same way otherwise it won't work. Email should be a valuable tool for the business, not a place people come and get overwhelmed.

Facebook and other social media platforms

Social media has become part of life and business. It's how we stay in touch, get updates on our family, friends and clients and where we hang out when we cannot be together. Businesses in the last decade have invested a lot of their time and money mastering social media as the main platform to advertise and promote their products and services. With the development of new social media platforms and the need to be posting frequently, VAs have started to play a massive part in supporting business owners by posting on their behalf and managing all the various social media platforms. This alone could be the job of one VA. It is very time consuming yet super important that as a business owner you have a social media presence. Here I will explain how we use social media and how Lendy is involved.

- **Community building** – we have a few groups that we facilitate where different levels of clients hang out. Our public group with 15,000 members Ultimate Business Support, our author specific group of 2000 members called Author Your Way to Riches and our secret group with private high paying clients Ultimate 48 Hour Author Mastermind with around 400 members at the time of writing this book. We post, nurture and provide support collectively via these groups. Lendy follows the posts, responds to things she knows how to, reminds clients of our events, welcomes new members and deletes any inappropriate posts. Unless it's an announcement or an update I have asked Lendy to post, she doesn't create any new content. Myself and my husband Stuart always curate new content that she can use with images and spread all over other groups and other platforms. We want to ensure that our voice and style is captured in these posts for consistency and branding. Some VAs, however, are required to research and write content pieces on the business and you will need to figure out if this is a strength of your VA that can be utilised.

- **Client interaction** – we often set up secret messenger threads for specific groups of people (e.g. retreat group, group book launch group, masterclass group). In these private messages, Lendy helps the clients with any questions on that specific event and manages and coordinates what she needs to ensure the event ends up running smoothly at our end.

- **Adding value** – when we curate new content, Lendy is responsible for sharing it and posting it in various groups and other platforms for more exposure and relationship building.

- **Business promotions** – once we have been adding value to various groups and in different places, we know it's ok to put up an offer or a promotion that will be received well by the members of that group. We also encourage Lendy to share these offers everywhere and this is where some of her incentives come from. If people take up the offer or buy the product, she will get a % or $ amount from that sale.

What not to use Facebook for: Stay away from talking to your VA via Messenger on Facebook. It is quick but it's not a proper team communication platform. You cannot search for things shared in the past and any images shared are significantly reduced in resolution by Facebook. We used it like this for the first few years but discovered a much more professional platform in Slack that does it a lot better than Messenger. More on this soon.

Also, do your best to keep your clients away from Messenger. Encourage email communication at all times unless it's something more social, fun or they are sharing a win or an update that doesn't need a servicing action. For me it got out of hand, so I created these two messages and updates for my team that I get Lendy to use:

When someone sends me a Facebook message that requires a business servicing action:

Hey,

Thanks for your message. Could I please ask you to send me this message as an email to book@ultimate48hourauthor.com.au

Sometimes when I look at messages in Messenger, I cannot respond in the moment. There is a chance I may forget to respond to you, as the message will appear as read at my end. Via email, you are also more likely to get a faster response if your question can be answered by someone else on the team who also sees your email.

When it comes to emails, they never get deleted until they are responded to and our inbox is cleared every single business day. I trust you understand. Thanks!

Nat ☺

When we wanted to change being contacted on Messenger all the time:

Subject Line: IMPORTANT! New communication style with the Ultimate 48 Hour Author Team

Hey Authors,

Hope you are doing well. This email is going out to our active clients from the past six months and all upcoming retreat attendees. The team and I would like to communicate a more streamlined process for the communication between us. We have found lately that we are getting messages from the same individual in 4–5 places and thus the communication flow is spread, scattered and sometimes we double up answering you if two team members pick up the same message.

Moving forward we kindly request that all communication gets moved to email only. Facebook can still be used and is great for logistics pre retreat, bonding, sharing wins, fun stuff and the interactions we have in the group and socially. Where it becomes challenging is when multiple messages are started, e.g. Nat, Nik and Author, Nat, Stu and Author, Nat, Stu, Viv and Author, Nat & Author. Add emails to that and we have five locations to track information in. Also, if I see your Messenger message and I'm unable to respond in the moment, there is a chance we may forget to return to it later if it no longer appears new in Messenger.

As all of you would attest to, we love being prompt in responding and getting back to you. In the nine years of business, no-one has ever said we did not return a message to them in a reasonable time frame, often at nights, weekends and holidays.

Having all questions sent on email also means that your email will be seen by the team (not just one person) and is more likely to be responded to faster.

Although, I like to clear my inbox at the end of every day, there are times I also want to unplug and may decide to leave it till Monday if it's the weekend. This will not happen in normal business hours ever.

The benefit of emailing is that no email ever gets deleted until it is responded to. In the unlikely event that your email may not get an answer, I suggest resending it or texting us to see if it reached us. Some emails very rarely have ended up in spam or junk. I suggest texting/calling if there is something super urgent.

Finally, here is a brief overview of who is responsible for what in the team:

STU – Pre retreat prep work, blurb feedback, mentorship on content, marketing enquiries, mindset, copywriting

NAT – All publishing matters, mentorship, financials, design feedback

VIV – All publishing matters, follow-up and accountability, time lines, techy support, customer service

LENDY – Event logistics and coordination of events

Thank you so much for your cooperation and helping us streamline this process.

Warm regards,
Signature here

The last thing I am going to say about social media is to be very mindful not to get stuck in the vortex of it all. It's one of the biggest time suckers. Get in and get out 2–3 times a day and outsource the rest to your VA to do.

YouTube

Even though YouTube is yet another social media platform, it deserves its own section as we also use it as a membership area for our business. Over the 10 years I have been in business, I have been uploading content and videos on YouTube pretty much weekly. Nowadays I have more than 1000 videos on there and continue to grow my content base weekly. Lendy is always downloading any live streams I do on Facebook and putting them up as videos on YouTube. This way we are sharing valuable free content on multiple platforms and getting a lot more exposure then just the live audience at the time. She also extracts the audio from these videos and posts it as a podcast on a platform called Anchor FM.

Another feature of YouTube is the ability to list videos as public, unlisted or private. By making some of my content for my private clients unlisted, I have been able to create unlisted playlists that I only share with my paying clients. That way, by simply sharing a link with them (that is the only way you can view an unlisted video) they can get access to hundreds of hours of training content to help them leverage and market their business and books. With the help of Lendy we have neatly organised all these videos and have a document file with all the links that we give our paying clients.

Lendy also has learnt how to do simple editing on testimonial videos that we regularly get, so she does those for me after each retreat or event and posts them out publicly on my YouTube channel. When someone wants to see our testimonials, we simply share one single link that takes them to the playlist that contains hundreds.

It is really important that your VA gets familiar with YouTube and learns some aspect of simple video editing. Every single business should be doing video no matter what they do.

Dropbox

Gone are the days where we send files via email attachments all the time. With the ability to put stuff on the cloud, storage and sharing platforms such as Dropbox, Google Docs and iCloud should be the only way that you store your precious files for your life and business. I am amazed at how many of my clients still don't know this and I am the one to help them make that transition. By storing everything on a cloud-based platform such as Dropbox, you can then access those files from any computer or device anywhere in the world. Others, like your VA, can share those files with you and make amendments as needed. You can use these platforms to share certain folders with your clients and others that you collaborate with.

On day one I asked Lendy to open a Dropbox account and we started sharing a folder. This folder has now grown really big with so many business systems and resources we use every day. See screenshot on the next page.

As you can see, everything I have for my life and business is under the Dropbox folder. Nothing lives in Documents. In this case, if I accidentally drop my laptop, I don't lose anything bar the laptop being damaged. I do a backup of my Dropbox files on an external hard drive from time to time for extra security.

Lendy has her own Dropbox on her computer and we only share certain folders amongst one another that are relevant to the work we do. Please don't delay setting up your files in this way before it's too late. The investment amount for something like this varies across different platforms. If you use Office 365, you get One Drive for free, or a personal Dropbox is less than $200 per year for 2Tb of space which is massive. I only currently use 13% of the storage capacity of my Dropbox and trust me, I have so many files. Photos and videos always take up the most space so decide if you want to have them on Dropbox or an external hard drive which is what I do.

A warning on Dropbox: If you are sharing a folder with your VA, you need to be mindful that only one person at a time is working on a file and has it open. Otherwise you can end up with two files (one conflicted) and some of your work may end up being lost. I have been caught out this way a few times, so now we always check, especially at times we are running our events, to ensure we don't have the same file open.

If you end up sharing resources with multiple clients as part of the work they are doing with you, make sure that you only give them viewing rights and not editing rights. If you gave them editing rights, you may end up having people amend the files or worse delete them. This would mean they will disappear in everyone else's folder that they are shared in too.

Zoom

One of my favourite meeting platforms that is super affordable, reliable, simple to use and has lots of functionality is Zoom. We use it for team, client meetings and group online seminars and webinars. They have a free version you can try out, but don't hesitate to invest the $10 USD it costs a month to have the full version.

Lendy and I do all our catch ups and meetings on Zoom. She can record the meeting when I give her permission to and the best bit is that I can share my screen with her to show her what she needs to do. She then watches what I have shown her in her own time as many times as she wants and uses the video for future reference as a business system. I will talk more about systems in a later chapter and how easy it can be to create them with the technology we have available today.

Slack

The best place to communicate with your VA will be via a proper team communication platform. For us that is Slack. It is a free platform with paid options should you choose to upgrade. We haven't needed to and don't expect to be upgrading beyond the free functions we can use on Slack. Within Slack you can set up different channels for different discussions and depending on the size of your team, not all members need to be part of every channel. Here is a look inside our Slack and what channels we have set up:

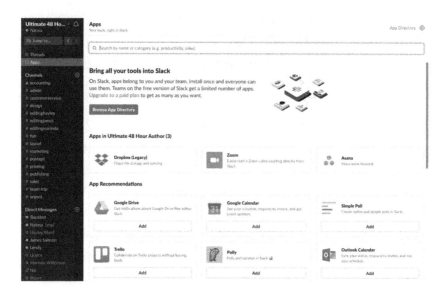

Even if you don't have a full-blown team, you can still use Slack with your suppliers or contractors for communication. We have channels for book design, graphic design, book layout and a few channels with each of our core editors. It is one place you can log into in the morning and see all the updates on the team. You can share files and tag those that you want to get a notification. It is very easy to use and even if it's just you and your VA, it's best to get used to using a platform such as this from the word go. We stayed on Facebook Messenger for way too long. Now our work is separate from our fun stuff on social media and it feels more focused and organised this way. You can still share fun stuff on Slack, but you have channels designated for that.

Asana

Like Slack, Asana is a project management tool and platform that is also available for free, with upgrades to paid versions too. Every project has many steps that need to be actioned and executed each and every time for consistency. This is especially important if the projects in the business repeat. Asana is also in a way a platform to set up more systems for your business. The list below gives you an idea of the kind of projects we have set up:

- New client onboarding
- Pre and post event tasks
- Group book launch tasks
- Retreat actions and steps
- Sales follow-up calls
- Publishing process steps and notes
- Client follow-up reminders.

These are the main projects that we repeat hundreds of times a year that need to be completed in the same way. Within Asana you can date tasks and allocate them to the team member that needs to get it done. The system sends notifications and reminders on the due dates. It also updates the rest of the team of things that have been done and notes that have been made there so there is no need to manually tell each other.

You can set up projects in lists, or vertically like boards. See these screenshots from inside our Asana platform.

Even if it's just you in your business, I recommend you start using Asana's project management tools. It will serve as a great reminder for you on what you need to get done. As you put on more people in your business (your VA being hopefully the first), you can start allocating tasks to them and they can set up the future projects. For us, I set up the templates and put them in the favourites area and then Lendy sets up the individual projects for all the events and clients as they come up. I really feel that she is the boss of Asana in our business.

Active Campaign

This platform is our CRM (customer relationship management) system. This is where all names, emails and mobiles end up from those that we meet, have at our events and those that opt in to subscribe to our communication. Your VA needs to know how to use this system and some training will be necessary as there are many CRMs and they all work a bit differently from one another.

Your VA may end up needing to enter new contacts in there with notes, set up emails, prepare a newsletter, schedule communication with the database and work out how to do autoresponders. Initially you may need to show them a few times how to do these tasks and ideally you should provide all the copy and content for them to send. One of the first jobs that I had for Lendy was to input around 1500 new contacts into our CRM at the time. This is also the first and only system that I had written. It kept her busy for almost two weeks until I created some more systems for other stuff for her to do.

As you can see, there are many tools you will need to use while working with your VA. You may not know about many of these yet, so you will need to learn them too. Be patient with it all, it doesn't take long to master them. We have added one tool and then another over the four years we have been working together. It's not about being perfect from the word go. Always look for ways to do things easier, faster and more efficiently so that you enjoy your work and so does your VA.

✷ ✷ ✷

Tips to help you learn and master new programs

The tools and apps introduced to me by the Ultimate 48 Hour Author team are all user-friendly. The Boss has a habit of creating screenshare video trainings, putting them in Dropbox and sending me a message saying, 'Hey Lendy, I have saved a training video in our Dropbox about Asana for you to watch and learn, let me know if you have questions'. That's it! Since the training videos demonstrate how it works with clear instructions, there are no more questions. All understood! We find this method is quick and easy. And before I ask questions, I make sure I have already explored the tool or app and watched the training video closely. I believe all VAs should show this kind of initiative and not just ask and ask.

It is also worth noting that exposure to different apps and tools widens your technical horizons. You become more tech savvy and confident as you learn different platforms. So long as you take the time to understand how the tool works, you will find it easy to manoeuvre, and you'll soon realise that you are already maximising its use.

Further tips to enhance your understanding

The best way to learn the use and purpose of the app or tool quickly, is to explore it. Don't just rely on the instructions, use your initiative and complete your own assignment so that you understand the tool comprehensively. If you understand the use and purpose of a tool, it becomes easy to play with it. For example, when I was new to Canva, it seemed very difficult to create images. But once I dug deeper, I discovered all the tricks.

Do not stop learning, make use of the internet to research and explore all the features. Widen your skills and further your creativity. If you know someone who is an expert on a specific tool, ask if they can spend a few minutes providing a short tutorial. But of course, with everything accessible online, you won't even need an expert when you know how to ask the internet. YouTube has a wealth of tutorial videos on pretty much everything.

You will need patience at times, because some apps or tools need lots of understanding, analysis or creativity to make the most of them, especially those tools for graphic design, video editing and sales funnels. These took me longer to learn, as I am not naturally artistically inclined.

Communication tips to get your message through clearly

At first, I was always hesitant to handle emails because I was using the Boss' signature and I was afraid I might provide the wrong information, or maybe clients would ignore my message as my language is far different to the way the Boss communicates. So, it was decided that we would all use our own email signatures in order to determine who sent or replied to emails.

Being from the Philippines, I am always very polite especially addressing clients and responding to their enquiries. For me, it is very important to address the query properly and respond to every email quickly. Acting as the events coordinator now, I constantly see to it that all the logistics information and instructions are 100% accurate.

I am always learning and looking for ways to improve my communication skills. For example, we once sent out a logistics email regarding one of our workshops that read:

*'If you work with a business partner or want your spouse to accompany you on the day as the value is always best received and understood when everyone has been through the experience, **please email us back as we occasionally have a few spots where we can accommodate a partner or buddy for free with you.**'*

We only meant for this line to have at least one or two additional attendees to join the room for free and we sent it out 10 days before the event. It so happened that two attendees of our event were actually business partners and had booked their tickets separately. They argued that if they knew we were offering free tickets for business partners, they would have booked only one ticket instead of two. They had a point, because the wording of the email did mention that we were offering free tickets for business partners or spouses. From that encounter, I have revised the line and only send it out if I see that we still have a few seats available in the days leading up to the event. The revised email now reads:

'If you work with a business partner or want your spouse to accompany you on the day as the value is always best received and understood when everyone has been through the experience, **please email us back as we have a few spots (due to some attendee cancellations) where we can accommodate a business partner or spouse for free with you. First in best dressed.'**

Another thing I always do is to acknowledge receipt of any email or SMS to avoid confusion that the email might not have been received and read. Also, when sending emails, I always tick the priority button and request a delivery or read receipt, so I can be sure emails have reached their destinations.

Most importantly, make sure that you always proofread your email, especially when it is a template email. A single wrong detail in the information can quickly escalate from a small issue to a big problem, particularly when you are sending emails in bulk. Check your composition at least twice before hitting the send button. Always use the 'bcc' field if you are sending an email to multiple recipients – if you use the 'To' field then all recipients will see the email address of each other which is highly unprofessional and is breach of privacy.

＊ ＊ ＊

OVER TO YOU:

1. Choose three new tools mentioned in this chapter to explore. Download them and start to use them.

2. Create a few screensharing videos that teach a VA how to complete a task for your business. These are the first tasks you will give them to do when you hire one.

3. As a VA that is looking for this kind of work, become familiar with the abovementioned tools and start to play around with them yourself. Don't be afraid to suggest some of these tools to your boss, as they may not be aware of them and it could make their life and business easier.

CHAPTER 5

TALK

Mastering the art of communication in your business &
How to communicate effectively as a VA

Mastering the art of communication in your business

Working virtually with someone requires the ability to communicate really well, especially as you'll be mostly in touch online where you miss the tone and feel of how things are said. You will have the opportunity to see and talk to each other on video, however most likely 95% of the time it will be via written messages. That is why, having worked with many virtual contractors and Lendy over the years, I want to empower you with some tips and tricks that will make life easier. I learnt them myself through trial and error. Once you become mindful of them, it will be a lot easier to work with anyone virtually. These points apply to your VA and others you will most likely be hiring to work with virtually.

- Remember written communication can be perceived and read in a different tone than it was intended – if you are sending something sensitive re-read it and maybe rewrite it if it seems harsh.

- Over-communicate rather than under-communicate – I have found that you really need to give super detailed information to those doing work for you. They are not inside your head and cannot know exactly how you want it. Write it out in steps or bullet points that cover every single detail. You will know when you are doing it right as you will get the outcomes you want.

- Use video calls or videos to describe what you want – if you feel you are getting nowhere, jump on a quick video call on Zoom and share your screen to explain exactly what you want. It's best to always use Zoom for more complicated stuff.

- Sketch – if it is a graphic design kind of thing that you are after and the designer is not understanding what you want, sketch it out, take a photo and send them your idea. It doesn't have to be perfect (they will do that), you just have to help them see what is inside your head.

- Don't give up in the early days – when you first work with someone, it can feel frustrating that they don't get you. Like anything new, it will be awkward. Stick out this teething period and the good times will roll on after that.

- Be patient – this is the most important one to remember. I have found people working virtually have developed this skill well and are doing the best they can to make you happy.

- Show appreciation for a job well done – praise and give thanks for work completed and done well. You never know, this person may become a very regular person you engage time and time again.

Meetings

Regular meetings allow a team to work cohesively, share updates and stay on top of new things in the business. They don't need to be super formal or something people dread coming to. As your VA is not going to be working by your side, ensure that you connect with them from time to time. Sometimes, I catch up with Lendy just because I have not seen or spoken to her for a long time. Other times, we have a list of things to go through and nowadays we get together our team of five for full team meetings to catch up and plan out our way forward.

We use Zoom for all our meetings, and I get Lendy to record the call, so that if we cover something she needs to listen to again, she has a copy. You could also get your VA to write up the meeting notes after the meeting from the recording with the tasks allocated to each person.

Within our business, we also decided at our conference that Lendy and my PA Viv needed to catch up weekly for a debrief as they work together to support me and the business. They decided to have a coffee/tea meeting every Tuesday at 11am for 30 mins or so and catch up on the week ahead, discuss what is in progress and identify what still needs to be done. This brings them closer and on top of where things are at within the business. The fact they got to meet at our first conference in the Philippines has been fantastic as they feel like they really know each other now.

When you call a meeting, know the outcome you are looking for in advance. Come prepared with discussion items and be open to suggestions and new ideas on how to solve problems or innovate so that the business moves forward faster. Having five on our team now, enables us to be like a mini mastermind group that can solve obstacles four times faster than we did when it was just myself and Stuart. The support you also feel when you start to have other people in your business is also multiplied with more people and when great things happen you have so much to celebrate with your awesome team.

Conferences

Something I never thought would happen for my business is that I would host an actual conference for it. When I worked for a large optical retailer before I was a business owner myself, as a manager we were taken to an annual conference every year. They were fun, educational and a great way to build morale with team bonding activities of all sorts. So, at the start of last year when we had our full team meeting, I just threw it out there that I really wanted to meet Lendy in real life. We set some sales goals for the business and if we met them by June that year, we would all go to the Philippines to visit her. As we are four girls and my husband, we said that it would be just us going as my husband would need to look after the three kids back home as my mum is usually responsible for them when we go away. He also couldn't think of anything worse than being on a trip with four crazy girls. We promised we would have a full team meeting to update him on everything covered when we returned home.

So, as we achieved our goal a couple of months early, as promised I booked our flights and accommodation and we now had something to look forward to. At first, I thought this would be just like any other holiday, lots of fun, relaxing and enjoying ourselves. My PA Viv, having worked for many other businesses in the past suggested we come up with an agenda for our trip on the business stuff we want to cover off on each day. This gave us a plan and structure so we can do the business stuff and the fun stuff and feel very organised and on top of everything on our return.

The first few days we just relaxed and rested from our travel. As it was also the weekend, we knew we wouldn't be as busy with emails and business actions. We basically switched off. However, from the Monday for the rest of the time we went through our list of discussion points, had one on ones with each other and still fitted in other fun activities and more relaxation.

Here is a brief overview of what our agenda looked like – this ended up being a 20-page document once we expanded on all the points.

Ultimate 48 Hour Author Conference
8–18 October 2019 (Boracay – Philippines)

Discussion Topics:

- Review 2019
- Plan and prep for 2020
- Refine systems
- Discuss our culture and values
- Suppliers and contractors
- Training on publishing in detail (Nat, Viv, Lendy)
- Team building and getting to know our virtual assistant Lendy face-to-face
- Personal development (Viv – sales, Lendy – publishing & systems, Nat – new hobby)
- Risk-taking (brainstorm)
- Pricing (sheet for smaller services).

8 October 2019 – Travel to Manila.

9 October 2019 – Day stay in Manila exploring city, meeting our virtual assistant for the first time in four years – meet & greet, ice breakers.

10 October 2019 – Travel from Manila to Boracay Island and move into conference villa.

11 October – REVIEW OF 2019

- Bums on seats
- Sales figures
- Customer service – troubleshooting
- Return customers (publishing packages)
- Venues and half-day event
- % of published authors vs. attendees at retreat
- Resources/masterclasses (are they using it) – how do we remind them all the time
- Bringing in the new agreement
- Review the customer journey

12 October – PLAN AND PREP FOR 2020

- Stu finding bigger and better venues
- Sales targets and bums on seats for 2020
- Increase half-day tickets 49 to 59 and 87 to 97 for VIP
- Publishing packages goals, systems & servicing (upselling to the prep session)
- USA tour approach
- Product sales goals

13 October – REFINE SYSTEMS

- New templates
- Refine the publishing ones
- FAQ documents

- Decluttering
  - Computer
  - Desktop
  - Dropbox
  - Emails
  - Phone apps

14 October – CULTURE AND VALUES

- Fun Fast Fame Family
- Behaviour towards clients
- No dickheads policy
- Managing different personalities

15 October – SUPPLIERS AND CONTRACTORS

- Editors
- Layout
- Printing & cover design
- Facebook ads
- Collaborative partners

16 October – PUBLISHING TRAINING IN DETAIL

- Review step-by-step manual
- Amazon
- IngramSpark
- Printing system

TEAM BUILDING (Ongoing during the period)

- Find activities/ tours

- One on one dates (e.g. lunch, morning walk on the beach)
- Puzzle (bring one from home)
- Card games

PERSONAL DEVELOPMENT (At different times during period)

- Sales – language, objections, soft sales tips… (videos to watch)
- Publishing (review certain videos)
- Research new hobbies to try (Meetup)

17 October – ACCOUNTING/ FINANCES

- Xero approach
- Outstanding balances
- Chasing up system
- Look at profit and loss
- Pay increases (Nat to discuss 1–1)
- Suppliers fees (increase) program costs…

RISK TAKING – (Brainstorm during conference period)

18 October – Travel Boracay to Manila (overnight in Manila for homebound flight on 19 October.

The above agenda has now become a template we can review each conference and improve upon. When we got home a week later, we had a full team meeting with Stuart, who read the full 20-page document outlining what was discussed and everyone got to work to action what we had allocated. While at this conference, we even booked our 2020 conference which will be on a cruise for 10 days. Lendy will also be coming to Australia to spend a month with us and be in the business physically for further real-life development of her skills.

Here are some photos from our conference in the Philippines:

✳ ✳ ✳

How to communicate effectively as a VA

Since I talk to the team almost every day for the past four years, when I met them in person it felt like we knew each other already. But of course, the thrill, surprise and overwhelming feelings of excitement were still there. I can't believe we made it this far! It never, ever crossed my mind that I would one day meet them in person. Boss Natasa, Viv and Mum looked the same as I'd seen them via video chat, and I got a bit star struck at first (lol). They had brought me so many gifts from Australia, which we call here in the Philippines 'pasalubong' – in other words, pretty things that you bring home for your friends and loved ones.

The challenge for me (which I feared as the meet up was approaching) was the 'speaking English' challenge, which I had a joke with my co-VAs, because English is not our mother tongue. At first, I made my assignment to learn what they like in terms of foods, activities, sleeping, morning routines, culture and much more. I didn't want to be too forward, because I always consider cultural differences and individualism.

My observations, especially with Boss Natasa were:

- She is very observant and appreciative
- Very considerate and thoughtful
- Moves very fast, she gets things done in minutes (she's a machine).

In general, the team got along well with everyone. They were very easygoing and flexible. Mum Ljupce, also had this 'young vibe' attitude. And they all loved having massages and swimming. I joined in a few times too.

The importance of regular contact

Meeting the team, up-close and personal, created an infinite bond among us. No more barriers, just pure respect and a family-like relationship. I became more open and comfortable with them especially with Viv with whom I now share a weekly catch up meeting via Zoom. After discussing business progress and activities at length, we also talked about other things, including aspects of our personal life.

I consider the conference we had in Boracay as one of the highlights of my VA career. It was so fun and very productive for the business. Being with the team for eight days, I felt I was one of the luckiest people alive to have such amazing company. We shared tons of stories, learnings, experiences, fun happy moments and we even talked about our personal lives. We laughed at some unique things happening around and I taught them some Filipino words and traditions.

The Boss also gave me something to look forward to for 2020, as we booked and scheduled our conference to be a team cruise of Australia and New Zealand at the end of which, I will have the opportunity to stay with Boss and take part in our half-day workshops and retreat in real life. There is a surreal feeling that I still can't believe that it's really happening. I know nothing is impossible, but the vibe is just overwhelming. I am always thankful to my boss for giving me such wonderful experiences.

Open, honest communication is key

There is no perfect strategy or communication technique that should be followed, as every VA and employer are different. However, I think it's important to establish rapport with your employer and to always be honest and yourself. Be confident, and willing to work hard without supervision – but if there's something you do not understand, always ask for clarification. It is much better to ask than to pretend you know the process and end up messing it up. Remember, you are there for the betterment of the business, so if you need some clarification about the assignment, communicate this openly.

When something does go wrong and you can't find a solution, call your boss right away. Be sure to follow-up to make sure things were resolved. Never just assume things have happened, always double check.

OVER TO YOU:

1. How often do you plan to meet with your VA?

2. What platform will you use for your meetings?

3. As a VA, what will be your process to follow when things go wrong. Write it out and follow your own system.

CHAPTER 6

FUN

Incentives and fun to keep your VA challenged and happy &
How to grow in your role as a VA

Incentives and fun to keep your VA challenged and happy

If you are reading this book, most likely you have never had a VA and you are educating yourself on the ins and outs of the whole process so you can proceed with caution and be armed with valuable information so you don't waste your time and money. I commend you for this and believe wholeheartedly that you will be really successful with your VA when you find them. In many cases they will be your first employee, so you can really invest time and energy to cement a strong, loyal and long-term relationship. After a little while they can start to feel like a part of the family.

Even though they are remote, it's important to remember that VAs have their own life. Show interest in what they like doing outside of work, ask about their family, relationships with others and stay up to date on how they are going. Often in more disadvantaged countries, they may experience hardship, family drama and disasters from time to time. This is also what makes them so resilient. Be kind and understanding during times like this. You can feel quite hopeless being far away, but knowing you have their back is what matters most.

Introduce them to your family and keep them updated on some of the personal stuff that you are also doing. You don't need to share everything, but part of your personal life softens the relationship and takes the bond to another level.

Team bonding activities

When we visited the Philippines to meet Lendy, it was easy to plan out activities on the island where we were staying. Through non work-related activities, we really got to know each other's personalities and character – yet another level to deepening the bond within the team. Everyone was on a level playing field. No-one was more important than someone else and we all took turns in doing the chores for the time we were together.

When you are remote, team bonding activities may not be so easy to organise. It can be that weekly coffee/tea chat where there is no agenda for discussion. Maybe a more spontaneous chat on how things are going might give birth to new ideas. After all, creativity comes from spontaneity rather than focus. Another thing you could do is to have an online game you may play that everyone enjoys, watch a series on Netflix you can have a banter about socially or in-house little sayings that become part of your language and communication. We came up with quite a lot of sayings on our trip in the Philippines that we constantly bring up on our Slack communication channels which bring a smile to our face when someone writes it in.

This is what will build the culture in your workplace. Not just work and tasks but people and lives that you are a part of.

Incentives and upskilling

As you train your VA, at some point you will reach a stage where you want to reward them further and challenge them to do more. This increases their value to you and encourages them to step up and do something new. Everyone can get bored of the same old stuff and repetition. After all, human beings are always growing and looking to achieve new goals and better themselves over time. Your VA is no different. As you evolve, your business, how can you evolve your VA? Here are some things to get you started on thinking about this more:

- Do you find yourself doing some tasks that you think you VA can't do, but you haven't asked to find out? Learn to let go, do the most complicated stuff and systemise and handover the rest.

- Can your VA be involved in selling some products and services in your business online? How can you incentivise your VA for this?

- If you are the one creating the systems, could this job become your VA's? Maybe you provide the verbal training and they write up the system. This would also mean you can then check it and really see if they understood your instructions.

- Can your VA spend some time learning how to use a new tool that will help the business? For example, if they don't know how to do simple video editing, maybe this will be useful to learn, as video is something every business should be doing.

- Think about changing your VA's title. Instead of a virtual assistant, could they be called something else? Perhaps they do something that is specific in your business. For us, it was to change Lendy to an event coordinator as 85% of what she does is exactly that for us, over just assisting me in random tasks.

Get creative and mix things up for your VA. They really appreciate being kept busy, learning new things and being challenged. If you have found a great match, nothing will be too hard for them and they will impress you beyond what you thought was possible.

✳ ✳ ✳

How to grow in your role as VA

For VAs who work with business owners, their thinking must be aligned with their employer's. They should always be open to possible expansion and enhancements within their role and be constantly analysing the movements of the business as well as the logistical systems of their boss, to learn how they manage their time for business and personal stuff. Do not just focus on the tasks given to you, be proactive. For example, be on the lookout for potential ideas which could help expand the business or polish the business systems and share these with your employer regularly.

When the Boss decided to expand the business to include publishing, I was one of the first to know. I was happy about the expansion because it meant I will have more to do, not just for events and retreats but now also in the publishing side. I was, in fact, expecting it to happen, especially as the authors were constantly growing in numbers, and I felt venturing into publishing was really a great idea. At the beginning, I was leaving the emails about the publishing to the Boss and Viv, however, as the projects increased, I was trained and I am now involved in the publishing side too. I am now busier than ever.

During our conference in the Philippines, the Boss allotted several tasks for me on top of my regular assignments as a VA. I happily accepted these tasks as I am certain that I will learn more and it was another way to upskill. At first, I could not keep up with how fast they were dealing with the publishing, but now I fully understand the process and I am able to keep up. The Boss has now changed my job title from virtual assistant to events coordinator. I think this new job title is cool and fits me well. I am not only doing the event coordination and enquiries, but also assisting the publications coordinator.

In my experience, it is very important to always embrace change and upskilling. You don't only upgrade your skills, you also experience personal growth as the new challenges give you more confidence. You will also feel that you are actively participating in and contributing to the growth and triumphs of the business.

✳ ✳ ✳

OVER TO YOU:

1. Look at your business and brainstorm opportunities to further incentivise your VA.

2. What parts of your business and tasks can you give to your VA in the future once you feel they have mastered the initial skills you have trained them on?

3. As a VA, how will you continue to ask for upskilling and what do you need to look for in the business to help them grow.

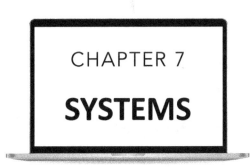

CHAPTER 7

SYSTEMS

Why clear systems are a must for your
VA and your business &
How systems make your job as a VA easier

Why clear systems are a must for your VA and your business

A 'system' is a set of tasks that are repeated in your business on a regular basis. Anyone can pick up a system and follow the outlined steps to achieve the same end goal. It is not creative. It is fixed until there is a review of it, upon which time it can be amended and renewed.

When you start out in business, you often wonder what people are on about when they mention the word systems.

I was certainly one of those people and it was not clear to me what I could possibly create that was a system. Until one day I started noticing that from what seemed at the beginning random and ad hoc, became a step-by-step way to find my clients, consult with them, set them up in my system and many other things that were being repeated in the same way day-to-day.

So, initially I started creating, bullet point lists and checklists that kept me on track, so I remained consistent and remembered to do all that I promised. My mentor at the time, encouraged me to document everything I did day in and day out in my business and how I did it. So, I began a journey of spending 2–3 hours each week writing out what I was doing. This came in very handy when I licensed one of my programs for losing weight – the Ultimate Mindset Success Program. Because I documented the steps of how I mentored and coached my clients, I was able to move beyond coaching just one on one and start working one to many.

This was great and the starting point of my understanding of what a system is. However, what I didn't do very thoroughly was document the systems behind all the other things, like how to find clients and actually run the business once you had access to this program. These are the systems that you must create if you want to give your VA things they can actually do. I knew I had to write up stuff and I held off way too long to hire my VA. The biggest excuse I had was, when I write more systems, I will hire a VA. This didn't happen for quite a few years.

The year I decided to hire Lendy, I had one system written (how to enter names into our database) and the rest I walked in blind. As she took two weeks to complete the data entries into the database, this gave me time to think up of the next lot of tasks I would give her. There is nothing better to put a rocket up your bum than someone else waiting on instruction from you that you are now paying. The same can be said for when I hired my PA a year ago – I always feel I work a lot harder when she is around than when I am on my own. There is this feeling that we need to get a lot achieved together and that we cannot slack off as we are investing money to have her help us, so we better get ourselves into a higher gear.

In this chapter, I am going to give you practical ways you can start creating systems for your VA that won't take you a ton of time, and some of them you can do on the fly to continue building your business.

Here is the short list that I will expand upon:

- Written steps (documents or emails)
- Screenshot videos
- Record your actions while completing a task
- Zoom meetings
- They learn and document
- Spreadsheets
- Training between staff
- Asana projects
- Automation
- Renewal.

Let's look at all these ways in a little more detail:

Written steps for systems (documents or emails)

The old school way of creating systems was to have them written out and placed in the policy and procedures folder of the business that was this gigantic binder that no-one ever referred to as it was too large and overwhelming. However, in today's world we can do it a lot differently, and there is still a time and a place for written documents as a system.

For our frequently asked questions we have a documented system of email templates, out of office templates, a ton of template emails that we send time and time again. We have folders in Dropbox and Outlook for templates that we refer to and use often. Lendy doesn't need to be creating written information, when it's been professionally written and created by myself. After all, I want our clients communicated to in a certain way and I don't need to be there, to release the communication if I have it pre-written to go out for every repetitive task and stage of involvement throughout our program.

Ensure that you give your documents names you will easily be able to recognise and find. Same thing goes for email subject lines. Once you start doing this, you will love the freedom of not having to re-type the same thing over and over again. Here are some ideas on what can be your initial written systems that any business can create:

- Welcome email for a new client
- Client enquiry for the thing you sell
- A detailed product/service explanation document or email template

- Steps on how to onboard a new client
- Thank you email after a client interaction
- Nice to meet you email when you meet new people
- Quoting template where you fill the gaps to quote prospects
- Financial statement email for you clients.

Screenshot videos

One of my favourite ways to create a system for Lendy, is just to record her a screenshot video on my computer showing the steps. It requires less effort as you are not typing and thinking and it's a lot more visual so it can be a lot shorter to consume by her and easier to understand as she can literally see it all in front of her. She has the capability to open the video on one device and do the work on another until she feels she knows it off by heart.

On Mac computers there is a standard program called QuickTime and that is what I use for my screenshot video systems. There are thousands of other programs that exist that can do the same thing. Microsoft PowerPoint has that capability too and even on Zoom you can record as you share the screen. Find out what is best and easiest to use for you and stick to that.

Each of my video systems are quite short, 2–10 minutes max. You do cover off a lot doing it this way in a shorter period of time. I speak pretending that it may be anyone else in future watching this, not just Lendy, so that you don't need to recreate it again unless something changes.

Save your system videos in a folder called Video Trainings and build it up over time by naming the files things that make sense. This is what ours looks like:

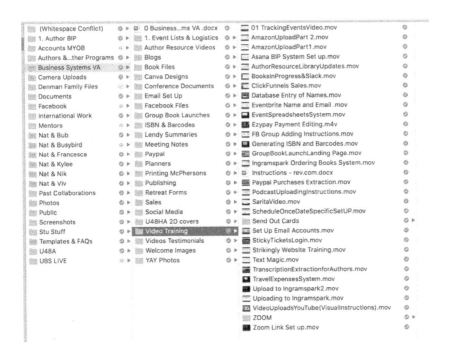

Record your actions while completing a task

Rather than setting time aside to film or write a system, why not do it while you are completing a task? That way you are completing the task that you need to do anyway, whilst creating the system to show your VA how to do it for you in the future.

For example, I was the first one that learnt properly how to upload our authors' books on the Amazon and IngramSpark platforms. So, rather than trying to create the system separately, the next time I needed to do this task for an author, I chose to film my screen and do it that way. It was a much better way to capture the system as you cannot do something fake in order to show the steps in those platforms. Not only did I complete the work I needed to, I showed a real-life example of what I would need my VA to do for me from here on in. All of a sudden, I won back 15 minutes of my time for each upload I didn't need to do myself and at any time in the future I can show this video to another staff member that can replicate the same steps for our authors. Kill two birds with one stone as they say.

They learn and document

Sometimes your VA may learn something you have asked them to do independently from you. In this case, why not instruct them to document and summarise their learnings for the benefit of the rest of the team? You should not be the only person writing and creating systems or training. You may need to when you are newer and alone in the business, but with time every single person in the business should be chipping in with this. That way, the business grows faster, expands to more people and gets to run like a well-oiled machine.

Zoom meetings

A Zoom meeting is the perfect place where you can also multiply your efforts. Sometimes I may be chatting to Lendy and realise I need to show her how to do something for me.

We stop and I allow her to record what I am about to show her. She records the instructions and when the meeting finishes, she gets the recording at her end to review and action. So many times this happens ad hoc. The key is to remember that the thing you are about to show your VA will be something that they will need to repeat, so stop and press that record button. Now you have had the meeting and created an extra system for your business. Boom!

Spreadsheets

Using spreadsheets to manage large amounts of data can help in keeping things simple and available at a glance. Especially if you are in a business that runs events, financial services or managing lots of clients on various projects and time lines. Learning how to use Excel is a valuable skill that makes everything a lot easier. Once you have your template spreadsheets you can rework them for the next project, next year or next client. I love all the spreadsheets Lendy comes up with to show me where our business is at with event ticket sales, event lists and tracking of our clients and their time lines.

Training between staff

Once the business expands to have more than two people in the team, encouraging training between staff members can reduce your workload and allow the creation of new and innovative ways of doing things in the business that are not generated just from your head. This is where the value of more heads bound together becomes astronomical for the business livelihood and how much it thrives. My VA and PA have weekly meetings where they catch up, update one another, have a social chat and develop new systems or implement training of a new skill. It's empowering for them and special to create a new type of bond.

Asana Projects

We covered off the fact that Asana is a project management tool earlier in the book, but it can also become a place you create and store some of your systems. By creating projects templates with steps, you are in fact building out a system for a part of your business. Further to that, at any time you can add who is responsible for certain tasks and by when those tasks needs to be completed. You as the business owner need to build the template and then your VA can copy it and multiply it across projects that need the same steps completed repetitively. Once the template is done, your VA should be able to take care of everything in Asana moving forward.

Automation

There are platforms that allow a business to automate some of its repetitive tasks. This is quite a sophisticated strategy that I don't think you need to worry about just yet. Initially, master the abovementioned ways of building up your systems library. When you do that, you can start to research a way to automate some tasks. As a simple example, in our business, when someone books a ticket to our half-day workshop, an autoresponder sequence of emails gets triggered which will communicate with them in the lead up to that event. I get my VA to do some manual emails as well, however the automation is there so that we don't need to do anything bar turn up to that event with our attendee list in hand. They also get communication emails following the event in an automated sequence that is set up via our CRM (customer relationship management) platform.

Revision and renewal

Once you have created most of your systems, you start to relax a little and think that you are on top of it all. For a little while this may be the case, however, you soon discover an easier way of doing something or a client asks a question you have never had before. Over time, you will find you naturally outgrow your own systems, at which point you need to review, rewrite and re-record some of them so that only the latest information and instructions are going out to your clients.

You will be able to recognise when something seems like it's missing. It could be an extra tip you want to add to an email or simply that it is time to refresh the look and feel of your systems – especially, if it is stuff that your clients can access. Be open to this evolution and when something annoys you, just redo it. Don't complain about it – change it and solve your problem for the time being until something else new comes about.

I find that we rewrite or tweak our publishing emails every 3–4 months so we can cover off stuff our clients are getting stuck with better. Other systems are around for a super long time and don't change. Usually the daily things you do, will tend to change more frequently as you find better and faster ways of doing things.

* * *

How systems make your job as a VA easier

All the business systems within Ultimate 48 Hour Author are well-managed. I don't have any difficulty dealing with each system as everything is made clear from the beginning, including its use, purpose and limitations. When my virtual contract of employment commenced, the Boss had set all systems up and put them in a document file – with log ins, video trainings, etc.

All our business systems are filed in Dropbox, and everything we are working on is there. All my outputs are there – events, templates, images, data, etc. We also have system emails set up in Microsoft Outlook where we can easily send emails using templates. Assignment of tasks is shown on Asana where you can put comments in the thread about progress. All of our internal communication is through Slack, which is easy to use and access. On top of this, we have our sales funnels and tracking, which I love the most, as every day I am picking up sales.

Our event system and meeting system (via Zoom) are two of the most established and solid systems that don't require much polishing. Our publishing system is constantly evolving over time, as we improve on how we do things. The sales and marketing systems are well-managed by Sir Stu.

How a VA can help a business owner build systems

VAs are always encouraged to suggest ideas to their employers to help build and improve the business systems. Having organised systems allows the business to grow, and reduces troubles and errors. With solid systems in place, if issues arise, the business owner can readily come up with a new refined solution. VAs should look to address any issues that may arise, and through analysis and research, come up with an idea of how to solve it or create a new system around it.

OVER TO YOU:

1. Write down at least 10 systems/processes you need to document in detail.

2. Use one or more of the suggested ways to complete the creation of these systems.

3. Give these to your VA and test how well they are followed. Refine and update over time.

About the Authors

Natasa Denman

Natasa Denman was born and raised in Skopje, Macedonia up to the age of 14, after which she emigrated to Melbourne, Australia to be with her mum. They were separated for two and a half years. She didn't speak English and found it challenging in the first two years to fit into the new country and culture. Her zest for learning and achievement fast-tracked this process and she had high performance results in her academic endeavours.

Natasa has a Bachelor of Applied Science (Psychology/ Psychophysiology), Diploma in Life Coaching, NLP Practitioner

Certification, Practitioner of Matrix Therapies, holds a Black Belt in Taekwondo and is a Professional Certified Coach (PCC) through the International Coaching Federation.

Being creative and writing books is something she never planned to do. Her passion for business and marketing was the reason she wrote her first book *The 7 Ultimate Secrets to Weight Loss* in June 2011. This book put her first business on the map and enabled her husband to join her full-time in the business a year later. She has also written *Ultimate 48 Hour Author, Ultimate 48 Hour Author (fully revised edition), Shut up and Write Your First Book, Natasa Denman Reveals… 1000 Days to a Million Dollar Coaching Business from Home, Fully Booked Retreats*, is a contributor of *You Can… Live the Life of Your Dreams and Speaking Successfully*, and is a co-author of *Ninja Couch Marketing, Bums on Seats and Guilt Free Parents*.

Ultimate 48 Hour Author came about as a result of the success books have brought to Natasa's business. Aside from books she has also written five programs and has three licensed systems that are being utilised by others internationally in their businesses.

She is now known as The Ultimate 48 Hour Author. Natasa is a highly sought-after professional speaker (CSP accredited) and Australia's leading authority on helping first-time authors publish their books. She has helped over 400 solopreneurs become first-time published authors in Australia, USA, New Zealand and UAE. She also has clients from 10 other international countries.

In 10 years of business, Natasa has been nominated for The Telstra Businesswoman of the Year twice and was a finalist in AusMumpreneur of the Year in Product Innovation.

Appearing in all major media outlets across Australia including the *Sydney Morning Herald*, the *Financial Review* and *The Age*, Natasa is changing the way people do business in Australia and around the world. She now runs a multiple seven-figure business with her husband and three children, travelling the world, spreading her message and helping small businesses thrive. Natasa's mum has now also joined the business.

In 2018, Natasa expanded the business and opened up her own in-house publishing company Ultimate World Publishing. This was a huge move for everyone as the business further grew to include the ability to offer publishing packages to clients. Natasa's clients are now writing their second and third books with the company, and beyond.

Hiring Lendy as a VA four years ago was a critical move to ensure the business continued to grow so that that Natasa could focus on further expansion and not the tasks that Lendy completes so well. Viv joined the team in 2019 as a local publications coordinator to help out with customer service and publishing tasks.

The Denman family's passion is to continue to build this as a fully-fledged family business helping thousands around the world become first-time authors without compromising on also living a balanced lifestyle. Their motto is Work Hard – Play Hard, whereby they work intensely for five and half months in the year, spend two and a half months on building new systems to add value to what they do, and travel and holiday for the remaining four months of the year.

This is what they want to enable others to create when building their own entrepreneurial ventures with the help of a published book.

Ultimate 48 Hour Author lives by four values: Fun, Fast, Fame and above all FAMILY.

Natasa's websites:
www.natasadenman.com
www.writeabook.com.au

Email: natasa@natasadenman.com

Lendy Macario

Lendy Macario was born and grew up in the Philippines, where she still resides. She came from a middle-class family, and as the eldest child, she strived hard to finish her college education through a scholarship to help her family. When she completed college and landed a job, she stood as a breadwinner of the family, sending her five siblings to school until they graduated college.

As Lendy believes that learning is constant, she enrolled into the College of Law. Fortunately, she was able to juggle work and law school and successfully finished her law degree without compromising her job. After her law studies, she resigned from her job to take the bar examinations. Determined to continue supporting her family, she looked for a job while waiting for the results of the exams – and there her VA career began.

Lendy is now a certified lawyer in the Philippines, but has chosen to continue her work as a VA at the same time. She can't imagine giving up her VA career with the Ultimate 48 Hour Author team. Inspired by the accomplishment of her Boss as an author and entrepreneur, she has dreamed of one day writing a book – but never imagined it would happen so soon.

Email: book@ultimate48hourauthor.com.au

Find Me a VA

From time to time, both Natasa and Lendy get asked by their clients for help in sourcing virtual assistants they can trust. As such, we do our best to see if there is anyone available to then create an introduction between the person looking and the virtual assistant.

This does create extra work and management within the business, however, in our experience having the right connections in another country makes for a valuable and safer way to find the right VA.

We are **NOT** offering an agency type of service, but more so a way to connect you with someone that will work out great as a VA for you.

How does it work?

1. Email Lendy at book@ultimate48hourauthor.com. au with the subject line 'Request for a VA'. In the email describe who you are, your business and exactly what you are looking for. The more detail the better.

2. Lendy will do some research and hopefully have someone to introduce you to that you can interview. She will do the groundwork to find a suitable match.

3. You conduct the interview and decide whether or not you will hire the VA.

4. After four weeks of successful employment of your new VA there is a 'finder's fee' payable to Ultimate 48 Hour Author who will in turn pay Lendy for her work.

Contact us to find out the current 'finder's fee' as prices change over time and thus are not put in print in this book.

Ultimate 48 Hour
Author Opportunities

ULTIMATE WORLD
—— PUBLISHING ——

Introducing Ultimate World Publishing – the publishing company that wants nothing more but to help you get your book in your hands with full control of everything.

We promise that you will:

- Receive your print ready files with no strings attached

- Be able to control the number of copies and timing of the publishing of your book as it will be on your own print on demand account

- Never be sold expensive marketing done-for-you packages as we don't offer them

- Get your book done super-fast (after all we run the Ultimate 48 Hour Author!)

- Have one dedicated team member work with you during your book publishing project

- Get to keep all your profits and royalties as we want to set you free after we help you with your book

- Have access to our amazing secret community of over 300 authors (so far).

Quoting on book publishing is difficult without a conversation. Specifics such as the size of the book, style of paper, colour, images and product finish vary the cost significantly from book to book.

Our **Ultimate Publishing Package** includes the following as standard:

- ISBN numbers for both your book and ebook
- Copyediting
- Proofing of your book by our editor post internal layout
- Professional print ready cover design
- Full internal layout of up to 15 images included
- Ebook conversion of your book

- Amazon upload of your book
- Print on demand upload and set up via IngramSpark
- One proof print copy of your book
- One lot of revised files re-uploaded to IngramSpark upon reviewing your book
- Australian National and State Library deposit of your book.

Call us for a 10-minute chat on **1300 664 006** or fill out the inquiry form on our website www.writeabook.com.au/ultimate-world-publishing/ so we can determine what your vision is for your book. We'll then provide a quote on a customised package that will enable you to publish a book that is the perfect reflection of your style, brand, and personality.

ULTIMATE 48 HOUR
— A U T H O R —

Ultimate 48 Hour Author Packages

	Done For You Retreat	Do It Yourself
Online Author Portal	✓	✓
Ultimate 48 Hour Author online course (12 modules + resources)	✓	✓
Weekly Q&A Live Calls in Secret Author's Group	✓	✓
Bums on Seats online course (12 modules + resources)	✓	✓
Library of over 200 hours of filmed footage on marketing & sales	✓	✓
Lifetime membership to our Secret Facebook Communities	✓	✓
Mentoring & Accountability	✓	
2 Hour pre-weekend prep session one on one	✓	
Unlimited email support	✓	
Laser mentoring until book release	✓	
Success Modules:	✓	
1. Leverage via Further Products	✓	
2. The Power of Social Media	✓	
3. Connecting Through Video	✓	
4. Free Publicity Generation	✓	
5. Automation Savvy	✓	
6. Pre-Launch Campaign	✓	
7. Your Mindset Success	✓	
8. Transcription of Your Book - 5 Hours Max	✓	
9. Checklists, Templates & Guides for Your Success	✓	
Retreat Package	✓	
Luxury accommodation – 2 nights	✓	
Restaurant style meals	✓	
Publishing Package	✓	
ISBN/Barcode for both book and ebook	✓	
Copyediting and proofing (40 000 words max)	✓	
Internal layout & design (15 images total included)	✓	
Mock-up cover creation for pre-launch	✓	
Professional final cover design	✓	
300 books (colour cover, black and white internal printing)	✓	
Ebook version of your book	✓	
Amazon upload of your book	✓	
IngramSpark upload print on demand set up	✓	
National and state library deposit	✓	
Online Masterclasses (6 Days per Year)	✓	
Speak for Profit (9-5)	✓	
Social Media (9-5)	✓	
Bums on Seats (9-5)	✓	
Products for Profit (9-5)	✓	
Technology & Marketing (9-5)	✓	
Sales Mastery (9-5)		

www.writeabook.com.au

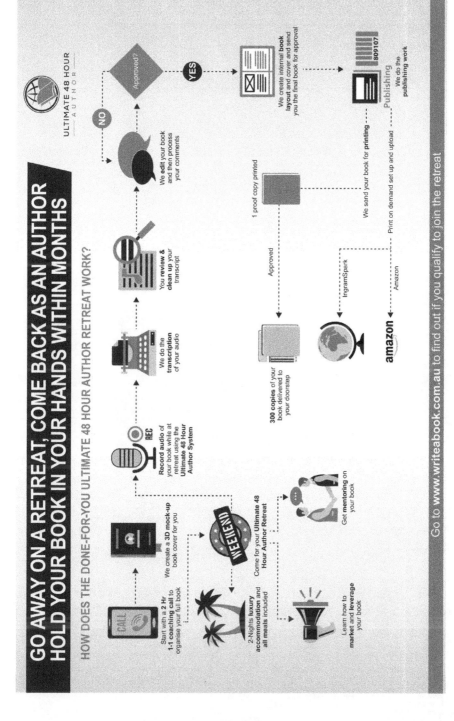

GO AWAY ON A RETREAT, COME BACK AS AN AUTHOR HOLD YOUR BOOK IN YOUR HANDS WITHIN MONTHS

ULTIMATE 48 HOUR AUTHOR

HOW DOES THE DONE-FOR-YOU ULTIMATE 48 HOUR AUTHOR RETREAT WORK?

Start with a 2 Hr 1:1 coaching call to organise your full book

We create a 3D mock-up book cover for you

Come for your Ultimate 48 Hour Author Retreat

2-Nights luxury accommodation and all meals included

Get mentoring on your book

Learn how to market and leverage your book

REC
Record audio of your book while at retreat using the Ultimate 48 Hour Author System

We do the transcription of your audio

You review & clean up your transcript

We edit your book and then process your comments

Approved?

NO

YES

We create internal book layout and cover and send you the final book for approval

809107

Publishing
We do the publishing work

1 proof copy printed

Approved

300 copies of your book delivered to your doorstep

IngramSpark

amazon

We send your book for printing

Print on demand set up and upload

Amazon

Go to www.writeabook.com.au to find out if you qualify to join the retreat

121